IN THE HEADLINES

Spy Games

CRACKING GOVERNMENT SECRETS

THE NEW YORK TIMES EDITORIAL STAFF

Published in 2021 by New York Times Educational Publishing
in association with The Rosen Publishing Group, Inc.
29 East 21st Street, New York, NY 10010

First Edition

The New York Times
Caroline Que: Editorial Director, Book Development
Phyllis Collazo: Photo Rights/Permissions Editor
Heidi Giovine: Administrative Manager

Rosen Publishing
Megan Kellerman: Managing Editor
Xina M. Uhl: Editor
Greg Tucker: Creative Director
Brian Garvey: Art Director

Cataloging-in-Publication Data
Names: New York Times Company.
Title: Spy games: cracking government secrets / edited by the
New York Times editorial staff.
Description: New York : The New York Times Educational Publishing,
2020. | Series: In the headlines | Includes glossary and index.
Identifiers: ISBN 9781642823516 (library bound) | ISBN
9781642823509 (pbk.) | ISBN 9781642823523 (ebook)
Subjects: LCSH: Spies—Juvenile literature. | Espionage—
Juvenile literature. | Cryptography—Juvenile literature. |
Intelligence service—Juvenile literature. | Military intelligence—
Juvenile literature.
Classification: LCC UB270.5 S654 2020 | DDC 327.1209'045—dc23

Manufactured in the United States of America

On the cover: Kryptos is a sculpture made out of code. It sits
on the grounds of the C.I.A. headquarters in Virginia; Carol M.
Highsmith/Buyenlarge/Getty Images.

Contents

1940–1979: World War II and the Cold War

1980–1999: Dawn of the Computer Age

CHAPTER 5

2000–Present: Challenges of the 21st Century

Introduction

WHENEVER PEOPLE HAVE interests or goals at odds with others, secrets abound. Where there are secrets, there are inevitably spies who seek them out for their own benefit, whether that is for their own country or group, or just their own wallets. Espionage is, by its very nature, dangerous. That may be part of its appeal to thrill seekers and consumers of spy novels and movies, but throughout the centuries spies have often paid for their activities with their lives.

Wars between and within nations are the most obvious users of spies. Before the instant communication provided by today's cell phones and internet, it could take days or even months to relay information about troop movements, battle outcomes, executive decisions and more to the military. The Civil War period demonstrated how useful spies could be for these purposes and for the sabotaging of enemy forces. The devastating loss of life incurred by both sides during the Civil War may have made government officials and military commanders quick to execute suspected spies. Other significant wars also saw an upsurge in spy activity: World War I, World War II and the decades-long struggle known as the Cold War. Notable figures such as Mata Hari and Julius and Ethel Rosenberg became notorious as spies.

Just as common as the use of spies are the efforts to protect their identities and keep their information secret through disguises and secret codes. Codes can be as simple as handwritten ciphers or as sophisticated as the World War II Enigma machine. During World War II, American intelligence officers made use of the Navajo language to communicate information by code. The language, developed over time by this southwestern U.S. Native American tribe provided

The National Cryptologic Museum in Annapolis Junction, Md., has two Enigma machines from Nazi Germany on display.

an unbreakable code. The efforts of many code breakers only became known after the war's end.

While war may be the most obvious occupation of spies, it is not the only one. Criminal organizations, crime fighters and political promoters have also used spies and counterspies.

Into the 1960s, the United States' efforts to conquer outer space by sending men to the moon and beyond jump-started computer use and technology in previously unimaginable ways. Later, private companies seized on these developments to create internet applications and devices such as cell phones. The use of these powerful new tools opened up new channels for governments to spy on people and for thieves to access the bank accounts and other personal data of many everyday users.

Today, museum exhibitions and book reviews examine the history of espionage and code breaking. Codes and code breaking are an integral part of security, including national security. Newly developed computer tools are being used to keep or break the secrets of governments, including those of the Chinese government, whose interests, both political and economic, are often at odds with those of the United States. In addition, news reports have detailed Russian efforts to interfere in the 2016 U.S. elections, and two former Twitter employees in the United States have been charged with spying for Saudi Arabia. As we continue on into the digital age, the tools and strategies of spies and code breakers alike grow more sophisticated by the day.

CHAPTER 1

1852–1899: War and Foreign Threats

Beset by the Civil War (1861–1865), this period demonstrates how concerned the country was with spies and saboteurs. Those who were caught often paid with their lives. Codes were sent in secret military communications, and there were reports of a male spy disguising himself as a woman. Domestic espionage remained a public concern even decades after the Civil War ended.

The Inventor of the Code of Army Signals

BY THE NEW YORK TIMES | FEB. 14, 1862

IN A DETAILED DESCRIPTION of the Burnside Expedition, which was given in The Times on Wednesday, a reference was made to the great practical value of the code of signals in use by the army, and the invention was credited to Capt. Myers, of a Pennsylvania regiment of volunteers. This attribution we have since found reason to believe incorrect. It was Mr. Frederick P. Barnard, formerly of Albany, who, after years of painful study, elaborated this very ingenious method by which intercourse, literal in accuracy, can be carried on at great distances, not only by signs visible day and night, but by sounds where the communicating parties are separated by intervening objects, or a fog. Mr. Barnard bears with him vouchers and affidavits of leading citizens of the State, attesting the merit and originality of the invention. It is due to him not only that he should have the praise his ingenuity deserves, but that a more substantial return should be made for his services.

Danger From Spies and Traitors.

THE NEW YORK TIMES | MARCH 2, 1862

FROM THE NASHVILLE UNION, FEB. 12.

OUR CITIZENS ARE WARNED against incendiarism by an incident which occurred yesterday. Cummings Doyle & Co.'s pork establishment was yesterday endangered by a quantity of chemical combustibles which was thrown into it while the people were assembled on the public square. Too much vigilance and caution cannot be exercised. *There are bad men, spies and Lincolnites in the city, who are ready to do any devilish deed to injure the city and assist their masters. The time for the toleration of even the mildest enemies in our midst has long since ceased. They should be ferreted out and forced to do penance for their disloyalty, or to leave.*

The man who welcomes Lincoln's hordes is an enemy of the country, and should be recognized and punished as such. He is the personal foe of every honest man and patriot.

The man who would assist in carrying out the designs of the enemy, should, if detected, be summarily dealt with. The time has now passed for sentimental charity towards such persons. Those whose sentiments would now lead them to welcome such an enemy as the Hessian troops, deserve no leniency from any consideration whatever. They are our wicked enemies, no more and no less.

FROM THE MEMPHIS AVALANCH, FEB. 17.

All the late movements of the enemy disclose the fact that they have received important information from spies in our midst. They would never have ventured to Florence, Ala., with their gunboats, if they had not known that country to be undefended by soldiers. Let a stricter watch be kept upon suspicious persons, and let them be summarily dealt with, if defected.

We echo the warning of our Nashville contemporary. Let every true man look out for the spies and traitors, and let them be dealt with summarily.

FROM THE NASHVILLE GAZETTE, FEB. 13.

It is said there are still some Union men in Nashville. If it be possible, that such white-livered scoundrels are really in our midst, our citizens cannot be too vigilant in watching their movements. Watch them! Watch them! Watch them!

Execution of Spies at Franklin, Tenn.

CORRESPONDENCE OF THE CINCINNATI COMMERCIAL | JUNE 21, 1863

FRANKLIN, TUESDAY, JUNE 9, 1863.

WHEN THE HISTORY of this most bloody war is written, few, if any, incidents will be of more thrilling interest than the capture, trial and execution of Col. Williams and Lieut. Peters. We had been besieged for four or five days by Gen. Forrest, our communications with Nashville cut off, and most of the time fighting, and were almost hourly looking for a general assault upon our feeble garrison. Col. Baird, of the Eighty-fifth Indiana, had made the best possible disposition of our forces, and all were resolved to sell Franklin as dearly as possible.

But last night the dull monotony of dodging shells was relieved, and excitement was carried to the highest pitch, as two fine-looking officers, dressed in what appeared the Federal uniform, and mounted on splendid horses, rode up to Col. J. P. Baird's headquarters, and introduced themselves as Col. Auton and Major Dunlap, of the United States regular army. They stated that they had, a few days before, been ordered by the War Department to report to Gen. Rosecrans, for duty as Special Inspectors of the Army of the Cumberland. That they had entered upon their new field of duty the day before, fully equipped and accompanied by two orderlies. They showed proper papers from Adj't-Gen. Thomas and Gen. Garfield, Chief of Rosecrans' Staff, and stated that, after leaving Murfreesboro, they took the direction of Eaglesville; and, when near that place, they went into a house for dinner; that while at dinner they were surprised by a party of about twenty rebel scouts, who captured their Orderlies, and came so near capturing them as to make it necessary to leave their coats and other baggage; that they were, unfortunately, out of funds, and wished the loan of $50 of Col. Baird, that they might go to Nashville to refit themselves before going further on duty. Col. Baird, although very suspicious that all was not right, felt compelled to recognize them, with such perfect papers from so high a source. He gave them the $50 and a pass to Nashville, upon receiving which the two started off at full speed in the direction of Nashville.

But they had scarcely disappeared in the dark when Col. Watkins, of the Sixth Kentucky cavalry, and Col. Baird both felt such intense anxiety lest they might have been imposed upon, that it was instantly resolved to pursue and arrest the two gents, and hold them until they could learn from Gen. Rosecrans the truth of their statements.

As no time was to be lost, the gallant Col. Watkins, accompanied by a single Orderly, started in pursuit, and dashing forward toward our pickets, luckily came in sight of them. He hailed them and ordered them to Col. Baird's headquarters. Undoubtedly the first impulse of these spies was to resist, which they could have done desperately, as they were both well armed, but the cool courage of Col. Watkins induced them to return. (Col. Williams afterwards stated that he put his hand on his pistol to shoot Col. Watkins, but the hope of not being detected caused him to desist.)

After Col. Watkins had brought the spies to Baird's quarters, Col. Baird and Col. Watkins questioned them very closely, but could get no clue to anything that would raise a reasonable suspicion, until Gen. Rosecrans telegraphed that he had no such officers in his Department.

The prisoners were then informed that they were suspected, and were under arrest until they could properly explain themselves. They showed correct maps of our lines, and seemed well acquainted with all the officers of the regular army. Cols. Baird and Watkins then searched their persons, and the first thing, upon examining the sword of Col. Auton, revealed the fatal marks (C. S. A.) — the die was cast and the blood rushed to the cheeks of the almost petrified prisoners. They acknowledged they were trapped, and at once confessed their real names, rank and position.

The Colonel acknowledged himself to be Col. Lawrence Williams, of the Second Regular cavalry, at the breaking out of this war, and was recognized by Col. Watkins as a fellow-soldier of that regiment; he had entered the Confederate service, and was now Chief of Artillery on

Execution by hanging, of two rebel spies, Williams and Peters, in the army of the Cumberland, June 9, 1863. Sketched by Mr. James K. Magie.

Gen. Bragg's Staff. That he entered upon this most hazardous enterprise fully aware of his fate if detected, but refused to disclose the nature of his business. The younger man said he was Lieut. Walter G. Peters, of Gen. Wheeler's Staff, and showed some excitement, but Col. Williams was perfectly cool after the first moment of detection.

Col. Baird now telegraphed the facts to Gen. Rosecrans, and received the laconic reply, to try the prisoners by Court-martial, and if found guilty, hang them at once, to prevent all possibility of Forrest profiting by their information. Now came the severe struggle — the prisoners had confessed their guilt; but to hang two such men of their rank was a terrible task; but Col. Baird was equal to the emergency, and knowing the exigencies of the service, proceeded promptly to obey Gen. Rosecrans' order.

THE TRIAL.

A court-martial was called by Col. Baird to sit at once. The following was the detail: Col. Jordan, Ninth Pennsylvania cavalry, President; Lieut.-Col. Van Vleck, Seventy-eighth Illinois infantry; Lieut.-Col. Hoblitzell, Fifth Kentucky cavalry; Capt. Crawford, Eighty-fifth Indiana infantry; and Lieut. Wharton, U. S. Engineers, Judge-Advocate.

The charges and specifications were duly presented, and the Court thus sitting, at the dead hour of night, after carefully and patiently hearing the confessions and other evidence, performed the sad and painful duty of finding the prisoners guilty of being spies, and Col. Baird, under Rosecrans' order, approved the finding, and sentenced the colonel, Williams, and lieutenant, Peters, to be *hung by the neck until dead.*

At 4 o'clock this morning, Col. Baird informed the prisoners of their awful fate, and could not refrain from shedding tears as he announced it to them. Col. Williams received his sentence with the most perfect coolness, but begged that, as his father had fallen in our country's service at Monterey during the Mexican war, he be shot, and asked mercy for Adjutant Peters, but as the order from Gen. Rosecrans was imperative, no clemency could be shown.

PREPARATIONS FOR THE EXECUTION.

After the sentence of the prisoners was announced, they began to prepare to meet their fate. They made their wills and wrote letters to their friends, full of the deepest affection and tenderness of manly nature. A Chaplain was called and the prisoners partook of the sacrament, and joined in prayer with great fervency. They did not attempt to sleep, but spent the whole time in either writing or conversing. At the request of Col. Williams, Col. Watkins took charge of his effects, which consisted of $1,175 in Confederate money, a fine watch and some private papers. Lieut. Peters had very few effects about his person — the only one of importance being a gold locket, containing a likeness of his wife, with a fine gold chain attached. He requested it buried with him, which was faithfully done.

THE EXECUTION AND BURIAL.

At 9 o'clock A. M. to-day, Capt. Alexander, who had taken charge of the execution, reported the scaffold and gallows ready. The infantry and cavalry were formed in hollow square about the place of execution; at 9½ o'clock the prisoners were brought forward by the guard. They marched with firm tread, and mounting the scaffold, took an affectionate kiss and leave of each other, when the halter was placed about their necks, and they were launched into eternity.

Thus two officers, who were born and bred gentlemen, one a regular army officer of the United States service, who had been nurtured and instructed by our Government to skill and position, expiated their crimes of treason against the Government they were taught to love and respect.

They were decently buried, and their wills and requests will be faithfully carried out, and here the curtain drops on one of the most sad and painful scenes of this accursed rebellion. Two men in the prime of life, with all the rank and position that talent could give, meeting an ignominious death at the hands of a Government they should have loved and defended.

THE OBJECT OF THEIR VISIT.

If the whole truth could be known, it would doubtless appear that these two men, of such high military rank, were about laying or consummating plans on a most gigantic scale for the overthrow of Rosecrans' army. Protected by the forged papers they had in their possession, had they succeeded in getting the countersign, on the night of their visit here, they could have marched a brigade of rebels into our forts here, and captured our whole command without resistance; but, if true, as they stated, they had inspected our whole front, they could have given Bragg such information as would have led to the most appalling disasters to Rosecrans' whole command. And when the verdict of justice is fairly given, in the heroes of this war, Col. J. P. Baird, of the Eighty-fifth Indiana, and Col. Watkins, of the Sixth Kentucky cavalry, for arresting and bringing those spies to their condign punishment, will stand very prominent. So gallantly defending this place against Forrest's siege, is a greater honor than a great victory on a bloody field.

A. V. B.

Arrest of a Supposed Rebel Spy.

FROM THE CLEVELAND LEADER | FEB. 19, 1865

A man in female attire.

FEB. 14 — On Saturday two young "women," apparently about 20 years old, were arrested by Commissioner Kirkpatrick, at the instigation of the ladies of the Soldiers' Aid Society, to whom they had applied for transportation to Washington, on suspicion that one of them was a man, which on examination proved to be the case. They gave their names as Charlotte Anderson and Emma ———.

The girl Emma states that she lived in Erie, but latterly in this city; that she had been acquainted with "Charlotte" some weeks, but had no suspicion that "Lottie" was a man. She is seemingly a modest and truthful girl and as there appeared no reason to doubt her story she was not put in close confinement but is at the home of Commissioner Kirkpatrick.

The person "Charlotte," when charged with masculinity, grew very indignant, and it was only by force that "she" submitted to the military investigation, which proved that "she" is a "he." He was looked up in the city prison on suspicion that he is a rebel spy.

Charles Anderson, as he calls himself, is very feminine in appearance, and has a soft and low feminine voice whenever he chooses to use it. When dressed as a man he has the appearance of a girl in disguise, and when dressed in tasteful female attire it is exceedingly difficult to doubt the femininity. His accomplishments are varied. He is a dead shot with a pistol, a splendid horseman, can talk three languages fluently, can dance admirably, play the piano, do fine sewing, embroider, knit and crochet equal to any woman. His statement is as follows:

The State of Ohio Cuyahoga County ss. — My name is Charles Anderson; was born in Hamburg, Germany; came to America about fifteen years since; my father is dead, my mother lives in Erie, Penn.; I enlisted first in July, 1863, in the Thirty-ninth Pennsylvania; left that regiment in July, 1864; being sent to Chattanooga by ———, I put on women's clothes, representing myself to Major Wells as a woman; he furnished me the clothes; I went from there to New-York City; I remained in New-York till October, then went to Cincinnati; stayed there till I enlisted in November, 1864, in the Sixty-ninth Ohio Volunteer Infantry; I was sent to the front; I stayed with the regiment till about a month ago; Feb. 10, 1865, I was out of money and was trying to get transportation back to my regiment; I called on the Ladies' Aid Society for help and failed; remained at the Burnett House, and this morning called on Clark Warren for transportation, where I was at the time of my arrest; I am a member of the Sixty-ninth Ohio Infantry, Company D; I adopted the course I have pursued to get home, and was intending to go back to my regiment; I came through City Point on my way home; I saw Gen. Patrick, Acting Provost Marshal at City Point; I told him that I was a girl; he told me to go home, and he told me he gave the Captain of the Provost Guard all necessary papers to protect me and pass me, that I might go home if I would stay there; I told the Lieutenant in charge that I was coming back; I was sent to the Sanitary Commission, and the State Agent furnished me transportation to Cleveland; I had a little money left; paid my way to Cincinnati and back home.

There is thought to be no truth whatever in the statement, as he appears to know nothing of the localities or persons of those places.

Certain evidence makes it more than suspicious that he is a rebel spy.

An Immoral Espionage.

BY THE NEW YORK TIMES | FEB. 5, 1880

AN OVER-ZEALOUS AND indiscreet agent of the Society for the Prevention of Crime has brought that organization into disrepute. Mr. D. J. Whitney, who is what may be called a law officer of the association, admits that he is at the head of a force of detectives, which, he says, "is modeled something after the old espionage methods of Paris." By this, we may understand that Mr. Whitney, acting as an agent of the Society for the Prevention of Crime, has organized a system of spies like that which prevailed in Paris during the third Empire, under which, if a stranger or a citizen fell into the hands of the Police, or was even knocked down by a runaway horse in the streets, there was always at hand a secret agent who could furnish the authorities with his name, age, nationality, and a complete diary of his life in the French capital. This system of espionage was instituted in the interest of a political despotism which suspected every man to be a political plotter and conspirator. In New-York, according to Mr. D. J. Whitney, of the Society for the Prevention of Crime, the system is organized in the interests of morality. Briefly, the practice of the bureau of espionage of the Society for the Prevention of Crime is to establish a watch on houses suspected of sheltering persons, male or female, engaged in immoral practices, and on houses which are used as secret places of assignation by persons of both sexes. Great stress is laid upon the apparent respectability and prominence of the alleged frequenters of these places. Mr. Whitney, in one of the interviews to which he has consented, dwells unctuously on the fact that the men whom his spies have watched are "prominent." They do not appear worth consideration and espionage unless they are prominent men. Having tracked one of these prominent and presumably rich men to a secret haunt of vice, the fact that he is prominent and presumably rich is next ascertained by "shadowing" him. To use Mr. Whitney's own language, "his name is got by various means, frequently by following him home." The information thus collected by the spies of the society is recorded in books. Thus the detective bureau of the Society for the Prevention of Crime has a directory of assignation-houses, brothels, and gaming-houses, and of the people who frequent them. It is particularly desirable that men and women of prominence and respectability, if they tread these forbidden paths, shall be snared in the net of the admirable Whitney.

The purpose of this system of espionage is the prevention of crime. The information collected by the detectives is not to be used except at the discretion of Mr. Whitney and other managers of the association. It is to be used privately. If certain alleged facts collected by this remarkable bureau had been used publicly, says the excellent Mr. Whitney, "two highly-respected families would have been disgraced." The highly-respected families owe their respectability to-day to the forbearance of Mr. Whitney and his detectives. If these estimable men chose to tell what they know, or think they know, somebody would be ruined. But they keep this curious information, as they say, for the purpose of suppressing the dens of infamy into which the prominent, respectable and wealthy objects of their espionage have been tracked. This is done by "a little moral suasion and a small whip over the heads" of the delinquents. These are Mr. Whitney's words, and we presume he knows what he is talking about. The delinquent is told that somebody knows that he is going to the bad, and that he should reform; this is the moral suasion. He is warned that the place which he frequents is to be "raided," and that he is to be called as a witness as to its character. This is Mr. Whitney's "small whip over the head." There is a peculiarity about the vice of the upper wealthy classes which makes it most objectionable to the Society to the Prevention of Crime. This is its secrecy. Open, notorious and flaunting crime is not nearly so offensive. When asked if the concert-gardens, dance-houses, and rum-holes of the Bowery were subjected to the espionage of the society, Mr. Whitney replied that "no respectable clerks, salesmen, or merchants go into those places except to satisfy their curiosity." In like manner, we must suppose, if one of these guardians of the public morals were asked why secret and mysterious haunts of vice are watched, while the gas-lighted parlors of infamous women on Greene, Mercer and other public thoroughfares, keep open doors, unmolested all through the night, from Sabbath to Sabbath, he would say that no respectable youth goes in there to his ruin. But this would be a frightful error.

It cannot be argued that rich and prominent men have any class license to practice immorality. But neither can it be argued that the "schools of infamy" are those exclusively patronized by the rich and respectable. Nor can such dangerous weapons as those contained in the secret records of the Society for the Prevention of Crime be intrusted to any man's hands. The alleged information collected for these records is in the hands of detectives and spies — men notoriously without character or principle. We undertake to say that no man of honor or refinement would engage in this most disreputable and infamous business. The spies are broken policemen, discharged firemen and dishonored detectives, who have long ago sold out their reputability. Mr. Whitney is undoubtedly an honest and well-meaning man. He will not use the black lists for purposes of black-mail or terrorism, and his books may be kept under triple locks and bolts of steel. Nevertheless, the information which he has collected remains in the hands of those who collected it, so far as all practical uses are concerned. No matter whether this so-called information is based on facts or imagination, the agents who reported it own it. Nothing but their destruction can destroy their ownership. Should they use it, as they may, no punishment visited on them can restore the character which they have once blighted. A man's reputation, a woman's fair fame, may be destroyed by one of these creatures in mere wantonness, and not all the torture which might be inflicted upon the black-mailer will ever undo the mischief which he has done. It is idle to say that secret information concerning the habits of respectable women and men will never be used except for good ends. This is the delusion of a zealous ignoramus. Espionage is hateful to a free people, no matter in what interest it is professed to be exercised. And the acknowledgment that such a system is countenanced by the Society for the Prevention of Crime is calculated to destroy the reputation of that organization in the minds of multitudes of pure and honest men.

Custom-House Espionage

BY THE NEW YORK TIMES | JULY 15, 1881

A spy is employed to watch inspectors and others.

WHEN SENATOR ROBERTSON takes possession of his office as Collector of this Port he will find a system of espionage in vogue on the docks of the steam-ship companies which is very annoying to the official Inspectors and Appraisers, and an insult to every passenger landing in this City from an ocean steam-ship. This system seems to be founded in the belief that neither the Customhouse officers nor the traveling public can be trusted. About two years ago a German who had been employed as a "runner" for the Pennsylvania Railroad to sell tickets to incoming passengers on the steam-ship docks, and whose reputation was not of the best, was discharged by his employers for alleged dishonest practices, and forbidden by the various steam-ship companies to come upon their docks. He was well known to Custom-house Inspectors and Appraisers, and they were heartily glad when he left. A few days after his discharge, however, he suddenly reappeared upon the docks as a full-fledged Government officer. He was armed with a document signed by Collector Merritt which practically made him a superior officer to the Inspectors and Appraisers, and authorized him to subject travelers to insults and annoyances which would hardly be tolerated in any other civilized country. His office was virtually that of a spy upon officers and passengers and he was given power to examine and seize the baggage of any passenger at any time, any place, and in any manner he chose, although it had already been examined and passed by a regular Government Inspector. This power he has held and exercised up to the present time, and it is asserted that in very many cases he has exercised his authority in an offensive manner. His ostensible business is to watch the Inspectors and see that they properly examine passengers' baggage. A gentleman who is conversant with the espionage system said to a Times reporter that it is the custom of this Government spy to question the servants of wealthy passengers and find out as much as he can of the contents of trunks and other parcels, and the destination of their owners. As he never wears a uniform this is an easy thing to do. Then, having selected a victim, he waits until the luggage has been examined and passed by the Custom-house inspector, follows it to the gate of the dock, and then, displaying his badge, rudely informs the owner that he is going to re-examine his baggage. Then the trunks are again opened, and their contents spread out on the dock. If anything subject to duty is found, no matter how small in value, which was overlooked by the regular Inspector, the entire baggage is at once sent to the seizure-room in the Custom-house. Not even a change of linen or a night-dress is permitted to be taken by the unlucky and indignant passenger. But in almost every instance nothing is found wrong, and the owner is kindly allowed to get his effects back into his trunks as best he can and go his way. But this, it is declared, is only the least annoying method the officer has of re-examining baggage. Very often the trunks are followed and opened by him in ferry-houses, railroad depots and even in the residences of their owners. A few months ago a gentleman arrived here from England with his wife and several children. He lived in the far West, and was anxious to start by the first train. The steamer reached her dock on Saturday morning. After his trunks had been examined and passed by the Inspectors he sent them to the Pennsylvania Railroad depot and went to a hotel for breakfast, intending to leave on an afternoon train. While he was eating the ex-railroad runner went to the depot, placed Government seals on the trunks, and disappeared. The gentleman was, of course, unable to get his luggage until the seals were removed by the officer. The latter could not be found until Monday, when he walked into the depot, opened and searched each trunk, and then blandly informed the owner that he could pack up and go.

Another instance of the ex-runner's arbitrary exercise of power was in the case of a member of the British Embassy in Yokohama, who was passing through this country on the way to his post. The Government officers had been notified of his coming, and requested to treat him with courtesy. They did so, but after his luggage was examined and passed, the ex-runner followed it to the end of the dock and compelled the British officer to again open his trunks and allow him to search them. Exactly the same thing was done with the baggage of the late Republican candidate for Governor of a neighboring State, who arrived from Europe in the steam-ship Gallia on her last voyage. A few weeks ago a well-known banker and railroad manager, who is also interested in a prominent sea-side resort, returned from a flying trip to Europe with light baggage. He was followed to his home in Brooklyn by the ex-runner, who demanded to be allowed to re-examine his baggage. The fellow was very properly ordered out of the house. Last Fall a lady whose benevolence has made her known all over the country, and especially to every New-York newsboy, came back from Europe with property on which she paid over $1,100 duty. After her trunks had been examined and the duty paid they were sent to her home. Then the ex-runner appeared at the house and endeavored to induce the lady to permit him to search the trunks. As she knew her rights, he went away without seeing the baggage. One of the most wanton and brutal exhibitions of his authority was made on the arrival of the steam-ship Germanic a few weeks ago. One of the Germanic's passengers was a lady who was dressed in deep mourning. When her trunks were examined no other mourning clothing was found. She explained to the Inspector that while on a visit to Europe she had suddenly been summoned home by the death of a brother. After a thorough examination her baggage was found all right and passed, and she had it sent to the Desbrosses-street ferry. The Government spy followed, stopped the trunks in the ferry-house and searched them, but found nothing dutiable. Then he coolly declared that he must search her person. The sorrowing and frightened lady fell to the floor in a swoon, and the man who had so grossly exceeded his authority hurriedly left the place.

It is declared by those in a position to know that similar outrages occur week after week under the present detestable system, and that they can be counted in hundreds since the plan was adopted. In nearly every case the victims are thankful to get out of the grasp of the officer, and do not care to make any fuss, which would subject them to further trouble and inconvenience. It should be stated that when smuggled goods are seized for non-payment of duty they are forfeited to the Government and sold, and a certain percentage of all sums received above their appraised value is paid to the person causing the seizure to be made.

CHAPTER 2

1900–1939: Crime and World War I

Codes became increasingly important as police made use of them to battle criminal organizations in the United States and abroad, though that use was not always without criticism. Political agitators and criminals alike used codes for their own purposes. The brewing of World War I in Europe caused concern as the United States struggled to steer clear of the web of alliances and entanglements there. The beautiful Dutch dancer and courtesan, Mata Hari, caused a sensation before her execution in France as a German spy.

Suffragette Cipher.

BY THE NEW YORK TIMES | APRIL 7, 1912

LONDON, MARCH 30. — Remarkable details of a secret code used by the militant suffragettes were brought out at the trial of Mrs. Pankhurst at Bow Street this week. They showed that the members of the Women's Social and Political Union had read deep in the literature of the political conspiracies of the Middle Ages.

The union had a special telegraphic code, some of the words and their significance being: Fox, meaning, Are you prepared for arrest? Foxes: How many are prepared for arrest? Goose: Do not get arrested. Duck: Do not get arrested unless success depends upon it.

Some public men were tabulated as follows:

Pansy...	Mr. Birrell
Snowdrop....................................	Mr. Churchill
Willow..	Lord Haldane
Nettle..	Mr. Asquith
Poplar..	Mr. Sydney Buxton
Lime...	Mr. Lloyd George
Violet...	Mr. John Burns
Dock..	Mr. McKenna
Ash..	Sir Edward Grey
Broom..	Mr. Harcourt

There were also code words for institutions: "Egypt" for the Foreign Office, "The Bank" for the Treasury, and "Home" for Scotland Yard. Among the other documents seized by the police at the union's headquarters and read out in Bow Street by the public prosecutor was a telegram of eight words which on being decoded read:

"Will you go to protest Asquith's public meeting to-morrow evening, but don't get arrested unless success depends upon it. Write back to Christabel Pankhurst, Clement's Inn."

Many of the names of the members of the union were designated by flowers, such as "Rose," "Pansy," and "Morning Glory."

From another document seized it was shown that $20,000 was paid in one year for the hire of halls and other places for meetings. The public prosecutor added that the accounts of the union appeared to be in excellent order, with all debts paid up quarterly, and with over $500,000 in various banks.

The Victories of the Spy.

BY THE NEW YORK TIMES | NOV. 3, 1917

ALONG THE WATERFRONTS OF our large cities the German army oper-
ates successfully, uninterruptedly, imperturbably. It scored its largest
recent victory in the Baltimore fire on Tuesday night. The destruction
of munitions in that fire was so large that it attracted for a moment
the roving, happy-go-lucky attention of the American citizen. But the
Baltimore fire was merely a large engagement. Almost constantly the
German army on the American front goes on with its methodical work;
a fire here, a fire there, and each time the work of an American brigade
at the front nullified. The Baltimore attack, perhaps, nullified the work
of a division. What does it mean to nullify the work of an American brigade? It means that more American soldier boys in Europe will have
to die.

What do we do with the German army of the American front? Sometimes we capture some of its members; we take in tow somebody who
has been seen "acting suspiciously" near the scene of the latest disas-
ter to our arms. And then we try him for a violation of the laws which
exist in time of peace, all exactly as if we did not know his object, as if
we thought him a reckless crank or a common robber and destroyer.
Keeping up the fiction, we send him, if he is convicted, to a jail to suf-
fer the usual punishment of common robbers or incendiaries in time
of peace. The German army on the American front records him as a
casualty and goes on with its preparations for the next engagement.
Tonight it is here, tomorrow it will be there; the Brooklyn waterfront
alone numbers thirty-two of them up to date. They attract no notice
unless they are as big German victories as the one in Baltimore, but
the tally steadily mounts.

At what time shall we give over the fiction that this is a time of
peace, that these men are ordinary criminals violating the laws for
profit or love of destruction, and meet the German army on the Ameri-

can front with the weapons which the laws of war put in our hands? By the laws of war the punishment for this kind of warfare is death. Not until we inflict it will spies and traitors take warning. The directing mind of these operations will not be daunted, for, whoever he is, is a German officer and takes his chances; but the tools he hires will. The spy from Berlin will go on taking his chance, as he took it the day he doffed his uniform and came to America to do this work; but the indigenous American traitor, the man who takes the German spy's money, will see things differently. He goes his road for hire. He challenges the laws of war. Enforce them. He does not believe he runs that risk. Convince him.

Spies and Their Congeners.

BY THE NEW YORK TIMES | APRIL 22, 1918

MR. NORMAN H. WHITE, a Secret Service agent, tells the Senate Committee on Military Affairs that there are in this city 20,000 alien enemies unregistered, propagandists, spies, drug-sellers to soldiers and sailors, mischief-makers to the extent of their capacity and opportunity. They are too many to watch. The Government has no control over them. If they are arrested, either they are not held or they get out on bail. They gain time. The Department of Justice is too busy, or not busy enough, to keep an eye on them.

The military authorities are powerless unless these enemies are caught in the act on a military reservation. The action of the civil authorities is uneven, sporadic, ineffectual. These impudent criminals too often escape justice. In the background looms that "wild justice," that tumultuary instant punishment, a danger always, a growing danger, as wounds and death come to our troops in France, as the temper of the community is embittered, as the laws are found inadequate or are inadequately administered. Every day brings the story of acts of violence, minor, fortunately, as yet, against the disloyal.

Attorney General Gregory has said that "the Department of Justice is doing all it can, but it must have better laws." Would Mr. Gregory be surprised to learn that the general opinion doesn't hold that his department has done all it could, that it has been too tolerant, that it has been feeble? Mr. John F. McGee, Chairman of the Minneapolis Public Safety Committee, says bluntly that "the work of the Department of Justice in Minnesota has been a ghastly failure." That is a harsh judgment.

Colonel Van Dieman of the Army Intelligence Bureau tells the Senate Military Affairs Committee that:

Great Britain and France now handle practically all espionage cases under military courts. If we do not soon handle them more effectively, there will be lynchings and outbreaks.

The waxing sternness against German sympathizers, against everything German, impatience with the German language and its press in the United States, appears in the news in each morning's papers. There is a suppressed excitement, only too likely to become neurotic and uncontrollable here and there. "The only way, in my opinion," said Mr. Lodge in the Senate on April 5, "to put an end to these criminal activities of organized German agents and spies is to treat them as spies and agents of that kind have always been treated in time of war. Try them by a court-martial and shoot them."

The so-called Chamberlain bill or amendment to the Sedition act of last Summer subjects spies to trial by general court-martial or military commission. There are differences of opinion as to the definitions in the amendment of the acts for performing, or attempting to perform, which a citizen or an alien shall be tried as a spy. It is surprising that there should be two opinions as to need and the moral effect of instant action in regard to these crimes of war.

Senator Borah is gravely alarmed by the bill, which cannot even be changed and accomplish what it desires to accomplish "without being clearly and unmistakably unconstitutional."

Mr. Borah asserts in the face of a continuous and depressing mass of adverse evidence that "there is practically no indication whatever that the courts of this country are not able to apprehend and punish crime" of this sort. No civil courts anywhere are adequate to deal with spies. Theirs is a military offense for military courts.

Secret Cable Code for World's Police

BY THE NEW YORK TIMES | JAN. 14, 1925

HEADS OF POLICE DEPARTMENTS in thousands of cities in the United States as well as in hundreds of foreign countries were supplied last night with a police code book which will be used in future for confidential messages between officials. The code goes into effect today.

Cipher experts of the New York City Police Department have been working on the compilation of the code book under the direction of Commissioner Richard E. Enright since a resolution providing for its adoption was passed at the ninth session of the International Police Chief's Conference, held here in May, 1923.

The code book is published by the International Police Conference, 240 Centre Street, of which Commissioner Enright is President.

In the book are thousands of code words, each containing five letters, which for use in sending messages to foreign countries can be combined into ten letter words, the maximum allowed by the cable companies.

The code is expected to provide secrecy and to effect considerable saving in cost of transmitting messages. As the code books will be specially guarded, there is little danger of information contained in a message leaking out to unauthorized persons.

Under the old system of sending messages from the police department of one city to another by ordinary telegrams, half a dozen or more persons would handle the message and be in full possession of its contents. Many criminals are expert telegraphers, knowing the Morse and international codes, so that they could easily read a message sent by telegraph. Sometimes criminals have accomplices within a police department who may communicate to them an important telegram.

By using the new code this danger is eliminated. A jumble of words such as "XPWTY, YFONG, SWING, PHSIZ," under the new code might mean "Arrest John Williams, 24 years of age, five feet ten inches in height, blond, light complexion, circular scar under right eye, tattooed figure of mermaid on left forearm. Wanted in Syracuse for bank robbery of $10,000."

In the same way a man who is wanted for a crime in New York may have taken a steamer for some foreign port. By using the new code the chief of police of the foreign port is made acquainted with all the necessary facts in the case and is instructed what to do, all in secrecy.

The saving in cost of transmission will be considerable, for with the new code messages that ordinarily would take thirty to fifty words can be sent in four or five.

Common phrases in general use in connection with police matters are described in a code word of five letters. Virtually every given name for a man or woman that is in common usage in English-speaking countries, as well as hundreds used in foreign countries, has its word.

A special set of code words for articles of jewelry, their material, style and design, numbering several hundred varieties, has been provided.

Besides the principal cities of the United States, police departments in Vancouver, Victoria, Winnipeg, Ottawa, Montreal, Quebec and Toronto have adopted the code.

Foreign countries using it are Siam, Chile, Peru, England, Australia, South Africa, Esthonia, China, Mexico, Guatemala, Cuba and India.

Spies and Counter-Spies Still Active in Europe

BY EMERY DERI | AUG. 4, 1929

With forgers of "secret documents," they thrive on the mutual suspicion of the nations. Here, a glimpse into the underground system when one is caught.

THE ROMANTIC TRADE of spying did not die out with the termination of the World War; it is still flourishing in our present era of peace pacts and amid projects for disarmament. Hardly a month passes without a dramatic spy arrest or a spectacular spy trial revealing the fantastic network of espionage and counter-espionage spread all over Europe by jealous and distrustful governments.

In recent weeks there were no fewer than four of these affairs. In Czechoslovakia a military court sentenced a Czech captain to nineteen years' imprisonment for having sold military secrets to the German Intelligence Service; in Belgium a lieutenant was being tried on a similar charge; the arrest of a Czech spy in Hungary brought these two countries to the verge of breaking off diplomatic relations, and the trial of Vladimir Orloff in Berlin discloses some details of the underground manipulations of the German and Russian system of political espionage.

Though these trials were held in part behind closed doors and the full results of the investigations are known only to the military authorities, they permit a glimpse into the dangerous activities of modern spies.

NEW FORMS OF ESPIONAGE.

Post-war espionage work is not done entirely along traditional lines. Before the war the trade of spying was nearly always of a military character, the sole task of the informers being to obtain data on another country's military preparations. The modern era has developed two new branches of espionage — political espionage, very seldom practiced in Europe outside the Balkan countries, and economic espionage, today an exceedingly important department of a well-organized spying system. Espionage has kept pace with the progress of warfare and it is today just as important for a General Staff to know what is going on in the chemical laboratories of a hypothetical enemy as to know its secret plans of mobilization.

What are those jealously guarded secrets, one may ask, which the secret agents of military Intelligence systems want to obtain at any price? For the sake of clearer understanding let us take, as an example, a hypothetical European country and the actual work of its General Staff. It is the business of the General Staff to be prepared for any eventuality. Therefore it works out elaborate plans for mobilizing troops in case of war, it builds fortifications in secret, it experiments with guns of a new type and it wants to know everything about the preparations of every possible enemy.

The news, for instance, that the government of a neighboring State has ordered the building of two new railroad bridges in a part of the country where only military interest could justify the investment might be a valuable piece of information, because it would indicate the way of mobilization and the plans for a possible attack. The exact design of a new gun, plans of a new fortress or military plans for attack or defense are worth any sum of money, because they enable the General Staff to remake or change its plans accordingly.

The possible opponent is also eager to have the same information about its neighbor's military preparedness, and because it knows that spies are at work within the borders of its territory it organizes besides its own network of espionage an efficient force for counter-espionage. And so it goes, until the whole Continent is covered by secret organizations for spying and counter-spying.

CENTRES OF ESPIONAGE.

It is one of the most difficult tasks to build up centres of espionage in various countries. Specially trained officers or reliable star spies are sent to these centres and it is their task to employ subagents and to forward the information they gather to the General Staff.

The most valuable work can naturally be done by agents who are in active military service in the enemy army and are thus in the position to sell the most valuable secrets. It happens sometimes that agents shadow an officer known to be in debt for a long time until they persuade him to become a traitor, but it also happens that unscrupulous officers offer themselves to the Intelligence Service of a foreign power. In both cases, however, the information received from them must be checked up.

The Intelligence Service can never know whether a foreign officer working for it as a spy is on the service of the counter-espionage service of his own country and has offered his services only to learn the names of a few enemy agents. From the experience of directors of espionage it appears that half of the agents are working for both sides.

There have been many cases in the last ten years in which clever work was done by agents without military education, or even by women. The Polish counter-espionage service, for instance, knows of a brilliant woman spy, who, they say, worked for the Czechs and could never be apprehended. In order to find out the location of new fortifications she watched all the newspapers of the country for official advertisements regarding field works. With the help of a military map she was able to find out where the new fortifications were erected and transmitted the information to her employers.

In the sensational espionage affair of General Radola Gajda, one-time Chief of Staff of the Czechoslovakian Army, two mysterious women figured as alleged intermediaries between the General and the Russian secret service. The charge against the General emanated not from the Czechoslovak counter-espionage, but from the French, who shadowed the Russian women and found them to be in contact with General Gajda, at that time a student at the French Military Academy at St. Cyr.

General Gajda as an important military leader of Czechoslovakia, an ally of France, received a great deal of secret information about new guns, plans of the French Army in case of war and other important data, some of which came into the possession of the Bolshevist espionage service. The case was tried behind closed doors in Prague and the only reliable information that leaked out was a brief statement about General Gajda's sudden resignation.

The work of spies in the time of peace differs radically from their work in the time of war. Let us take, for instance, the spectacular case of Mata Hari, one of the best-known espionage affairs during the World War. Discounting the melodramatic elements of her story — which contain more fiction than truth — we find that the Javanese dancer's main task was to keep the German Intelligence Service informed about movements of the Allied troops. Frequenting the company of army officers, she was in a position to learn important details about the regrouping of troops and she transmitted this information to the Germans. When she informed the German Intelligence Service that officers of a certain army corps were ordered to the Argonne the Germans knew that that particular army corps would soon appear on the Argonne front and they could draw the inference that a new attack was being prepared.

Another kind of information which she transmitted to the Germans was about the movement of ships. With the help of her friends she learned, for instance, that a certain ship transporting troops had left Tunis and was due in the port of Toulon on a certain day. All she had to do was to give the news to one of the many German operatives in Paris, whence it was telephoned to another spy somewhere on the French-Spanish border and from there it made its way to the German espionage centre in San Sebastian. A radio message from there informed the commanders of German submarines operating in the Mediterranean, who lay in wait for the ship and torpedoed it before it could reach Toulon. There was only one single case where she attempted to obtain information about the nature of a new weapon — the tank — but she was apprehended and executed before she had been able to obtain the plans of these steel monsters.

Mata Hari.

PEACE-TIME SPYING.

How different is the work of a spy in post-war times. Here is, for instance, the recent case of Captain Jaroslav Falout of the Czech Army. Captain Falout worked in the Czechoslovak General Staff and had access to important papers marked "secret." These documents contained plans for mobilizing troops, orders given to the Skoda gun factory regarding new guns and military plans in case of war with Germany.

First the captain went to Berlin himself, but later he gave copies of the original documents to a woman dancer, who traveled regularly between Prague and Berlin carrying with her the copies written in invisible ink. Had he not lost his suitcase containing secret documents on the occasion of one of his personal trips to Germany he might have continued his work indefinitely, supplying the German Intelligence Service with information regarding the military preparations of one of the Eastern allies of France.

Still more characteristic is the case of the Danish Captain, Harry Lembourn, who was in the service of the French espionage system. The Captain, who worked for the French during the war, spent many months in Berlin posing as an importer and succeeded in making the acquaintance of a number of German officers. A woman friend who worked in the War Ministry as a stenographer supplied the Captain with several important leads, which he followed up by either bribing officers or by piecing together bits of information. He was arrested when he attempted to obtain data about experiments made at Spandau on the construction of a new gun and was sentenced to five years' imprisonment.

Every year millions of dollars are spent by the countries of Europe on espionage. A great part of this sum goes to professional spies, that is, to men and women who make espionage their life work. Their qualifications are excellent international connections, a perfect knowledge of several languages and the ability to obtain any desired information. They almost invariably receive money not from one but from several countries, and their work is actually an exchange of information. In order to get information they have to give information, and it not infrequently happens that they sell their information to several parties at the same time.

The most important centre of political and economical espionage is Vienna. This is the gathering place of innumerable Soviet agents working all over the world. The work of Soviet agents differs greatly from that of other political spies. Their objective is not only to obtain secret political information, but to stir up trouble.

How these Bolshevist and anti-Bolshevist agents and dealers in secret documents work has been disclosed by the recent trial of Vladimir Orloff and his accomplices in Berlin. The investigation disclosed that Orloff was the central figure in an organization of forgers and spies having headquarters in Vienna, Riga, Paris and London. Orloff himself had once been a member of the Ochrana, the secret service of the Czarist régime in Russia, but he went over to the Bolsheviki after the revolution, then double-crossed his employers and fled to Germany, where he worked for anti-Bolshevist organizations and established a factory for forging documents.

The police found in his apartment three chests containing hundreds of rubber stamps, official Soviet stationery and every kind of material necessary for the band's work. One member of the organization had once been a cook at the Soviet Embassy in London, while another, a certain Pokroffsky, was stationed in Riga and served as a link between Russia and Germany.

Vienna is a meeting place of political émigrés from all over the world. An agent can meet here Spanish refugees, Communists from America and secret political emissaries of a minority party of a Balkan country. There are certain coffee houses in Vienna where one can see spies and Secret Service men from all over the world. There is an "exchange" for forged documents in the city, and twice within twenty-four hours almost any kind of "secret document," genuine or forged, can be bought.

SALE OF DOCUMENTS.

How far this trade in forged documents has developed in Vienna can best be illustrated by the story of Ignatius Strassnoff, an adventurer known to the police of every European capital. A few years ago Strassnoff offered for sale various documents purporting to show the details of a new Bolshevist conspiracy. First he offered the documents to the Hungarian Government, which refused to buy them. He then tried to sell the documents to the Germans and French and succeeded in getting about $2,500 from the first and $1,800 from the second. The documents were forgeries and it was Strassnoff himself who exposed the whole transaction and told the story of his deal in a Vienna newspaper.

The public generally credits spies and secret agents with the knowledge of more secrets than they actually succeed in obtaining. A real spy very seldom knows more than certain technical details regarding military preparations, and it happens often that he is not fully aware of the real value of such information. If a spy offers for sale a document of obviously tremendous importance, the well-trained heads of the Secret Service are liable to suspect that the document is a fraud. Really valuable information is usually of a technical nature, unintelligible to anybody except the trained officer.

The exact plans of a new gun are exceedingly important for any General Staff, but the average person would not understand either the importance or even the description of the plans. Sometimes it is a bit of information, apparently insignificant, which is desired by an Intelligence Service, and the spy who, after work of many months, succeeds in obtaining it does not even guess what significance can be attached to it. He does not see the whole machinery of espionage at work, only the details.

The system of espionage and counter-espionage in Europe tends to increase jealousy and general nervousness. Mutual distrust has gone so far in some countries that only trusted persons can buy or install radio sets and carrier pigeons are shot down because of the fear that they carry important news from one Secret Service agent to another.

So long as there are jealousy and distrust among the nations of Europe there will be espionage.

Mata Hari, Courtesan and Spy

REVIEW | BY FITZHUGH L. MINNIGERODE | MAY 11, 1930

MATA HARI, Courtesan and Spy
By Major Thomas Coulson
Illustrated. 312 pp.
New York: Harper & Brothers. $3.

NO GREAT WAR FAILS to produce numberless stories that challenge credulity and remind us again that truth is stranger than fiction. Yet it is very doubtful if any such sustained story of intrigue and espionage in which so many men in high places have been duped, in which so many thousands of men were sent to their deaths in battle, in which so many governments were interested in discovering the source of uncanny information supplied to the enemy, in which so many secret service agents bent their efforts at discovering the arch-spy; it is doubtful if there has ever been a parallel to the career of Mata Hari.

In reading Major Coulson's book we can only vote Mata Hari the most famous spy of the world's greatest war. For such a role she was admirably equipped — beautiful, sensuous, a liar, a lover, clever, and with a degree of aplomb that in many instances and in tight places amounted to impudence.

No one seemed beyond her reach and few seemed impervious to her charms. If she failed to snare her victim by one method she usually succeeded by another. Her activities covered a Continent, and she numbered among her conquests a French Minister of War, the head of the Dutch Cabinet, a Minister of Foreign Affairs and all ranks in the French Army.

It is quite impossible in a short review to begin to enumerate her manifold activities in Amsterdam, Madrid and Paris and a dozen other European cities. Nor yet to delve into the stout efforts made by the counter-espionage forces of France and England to focus upon her the light of discovery and then fasten upon her the guilt of espionage. At times she seemed the shadow and not the substance — although her "amber-tinted body" danced and wreathed before gay audiences and she was a popular favorite along the boulevards of Paris. The very importance of some of her victims seemed to clothe her with immunity, to free her of all suspicion; for some of her lovers were men upon whom no finger of accusation could be pointed so far as love of France was concerned.

Margaret Gertrude Zelle — for that was Mata Hari's real name — was cast for the unusual. Hers would have been a storm-tossed life had there never been a World War, for years before she had fled the gray skies of her native Holland and had achieved a reputation as an eccentric dancer with a beautiful body. She had captivated most of the capitals of Europe and she was clever enough to have attached some mystical religious meaning to the nude dances with which she delighted her audiences and won countless admirers. She was so insistent in her declaration that her dances were those practiced in Brahmanist temples and that she had learned them as a child in India that she doubtless believed, or almost believed, it herself.

The beginning of Mata Hari's undoing comes unexpectedly. She was in London and, while she was looked upon there with a degree of suspicion, the most diligent activities of Scotland Yard failed to fasten upon her sufficient evidence. Still they did not wish her to return to Holland, where she would be in constant touch with German secret service agents. She was granted passage on a boat supposed to sail for the Hook of Holland only to discover in the morning that she was bound for Cadiz.

She never again saw her native land nor the colorful East which she claimed as the origin of her faked beliefs.

The story of her court-martial and the finding of "guilty," her conduct before that court, the efforts of the old and distinguished attorney — one of her victims — who defended her and tried his utmost to save her even to the extent of appealing to his old friend, the President of France; her execution, with always the doubt that the soldiers were not firing blank cartridges and the whole gamut of her amazing career, all this reads like the imaginings of one drugged with hashish.

It is an amazing story, told in a straightforward manner, and one that mixes history, drama, comedy and tragedy and, methinks, a bit of fiction into a most absorbing whole.

Detectives Begin Cryptography Study

BY THE NEW YORK TIMES | FEB. 12, 1935

THE UNITED STATES ARMY has for the last month been training detectives of the bomb squad in cryptography to facilitate their work in tracking down the writers of kidnap and threatening letters, it was disclosed yesterday at police headquarters.

Twice a month Acting Lieutenant Charles E. Newman and sixteen men, who comprise the bomb squad, are being instructed by Colonel George A. Lynch of the army Intelligence Service at the Army Building at 39 Whitehall Street. The course of instruction is to be most exhaustive. Analysis of the various kinds of writing script, print and typewriting is only one of the many things the detectives will learn.

The many peculiarities of foreign types of writing both in English and in the native language of the sender also will be studied. A course in paper, inks, mystic symbols, perforations and signatures, everything that might help in detecting the senders of anonymous, threatening, blackmail, scurrilous or libelous letters, is included in the instruction.

Under an order sent out a month ago by Assistant Chief Inspector John J. Sullivan, in charge of the Detective Bureau, all communications, terrorist in content, received by the detectives throughout the city must be submitted to the bomb squad for study and analysis. The order instructs all detectives that after a first threatening note is received they are to ask the recipient to hold all subsequent letters without opening (so as not to destroy any possible fingerprints) and notify them at once. In turn an expert from the bomb squad will be sent.

The training in cryptography augments the regular monthly instruction in explosives that the bomb squad receives at the United States Testing Laboratory at Perth Amboy, N.J., under Inspector Harry A. Campbell of the United States Bureau of Explosives.

CHAPTER 3

1940–1979: World War II and the Cold War

News about codes and cryptographers was largely kept under wraps during and after U.S. participation in World War II (1941–1945), but in the 1950s Julius and Ethel Rosenberg were charged with espionage and executed for their crimes, a punishment that some today feel was excessive. The Cold War between the forces of democracy, represented by the United States, and those of communism, represented by the U.S.S.R., resulted in the use of spies and counterspies following World War II and through the end of this period. News about the wartime efforts to break Nazi codes by the use of the Enigma machine was acknowledged in the 1970s.

3 on Trial as Spies Open Defense, Rosenberg Denying All Charges

BY WILLIAM R. CONKLIN | MARCH 22, 1951

THE DEFENSE OF THREE American citizens charged with wartime atomic espionage for Soviet Russia opened at 3:45 o'clock yesterday afternoon with Julius Rosenberg, the most important defendant, denying the Government's charges against him.

Rosenberg is on trial in United States District Court with his wife, Ethel, and his City College classmate Morton Sobell. His brother-in-law,

David Greenglass, has confessed and awaits sentence. The fifth person named in the Federal indictment for espionage is Anatoli A. Yakovlev, former Russian vice consul here. Yakovlev fled this country in 1946.

As the first defense witness, Rosenberg sought to overcome testimony against him by Greenglass, the latter's wife Ruth, and Harry Gold, principal prosecution witnesses. Gold linked Rosenberg to Yakovlev, Greenglass and Dr. Klaus Fuchs, British atomic scientist, through a portion of a Jello box top used for identification between spies. Gold is serving a thirty-year Federal sentence and Fuchs is serving fourteen years in England.

Facing a possible death sentence, Rosenberg made a general denial that he had engaged in atomic espionage for Russia in 1944 and 1945. Tall, thin and wearing thick-lensed glasses, with a long, sallow face and a small black mustache, he sat back in the witness chair with legs crossed and hands clasped in his lap. He wore a gray suit, white shirt and a silver-and-maroon tie.

Before resting its capital case against the three defendants at 3 o'clock, the Government produced testimony on the Communist conspiracy here from Elizabeth Bentley, who has admitted she was a wartime courier for a Washington spy ring. United States Attorney Irving H. Saypol sought to show the jury of eleven men and one woman that membership in the Communist party provided the motive for all three defendants to engage in spy work.

James S. Huggins, an immigration inspector from Laredo, Texas, testified as the Government's nineteenth and last witness. He produced records showing that Sobell, the third defendant, had been deported from Mexico last August and had been arrested in Texas. This testimony went in over strenuous defense objections that took up part of two trial days.

Before Rosenberg testified, Judge Irving R. Kaufman denied nine defense motions. Two of these asked for a mistrial, three moved to dismiss the indictment, one asked elimination of all testimony on the Communist party and the Young Communist League, another contested the constitutionality of the statute under which the indictment was brought, the eighth asked for access to certain trial records and the last sought the striking out of testimony by the Greenglasses and other key prosecution witnesses.

When the defense protested that the acts of one person in a conspiracy were not binding upon the others, Judge Kaufman said:

What you're saying is that because the Government established with tremendous strength, because that portion of the proof was overwhelming concerning atomic information, that the Government hasn't a right to bring to trial under one indictment another defendant alleged to have conspired to obtain other secret information in national defense with intent to transmit it to Russia.

I believe I understand conspiracy since I have prosecuted a number of conspiracy cases. This charges one general conspiracy. There may be several branches, but they are all emanating from the same trunk, to get secret information. All have knowledge of the ultimate, unlawful objective; to get secret information for Soviet Russia. They are in the conspiracy even though they do not know each other. I appreciate your argument. I do not agree with you. And I deny your motion.

ROSENBERG GIVES HIS HISTORY

Under direct examination by Emanuel H. Bloch, his lawyer, Rosenberg told of his birth in New York on May 12, 1918. He said he had attended city public schools on the lower East Side and had attended Hebrew school and Hebrew High School before entering City College in 1934.

In 1939, he said, he had married Ethel Greenglass. They have two children, Michael Allen, 8, and Robert Harry, 4. Since 1942 he said the family had lived at 10 Monroe Street, Knickerbocker Village, where their rent was $51 monthly.

In 1940, Rosenberg testified, he was appointed from a civil service list as junior engineer in the Signal Corps, United States Army. His wife had obtained an earlier job with the Census Bureau in Washington, he said.

After recounting his education at public expense and his jobs on the Federal pay roll until 1945, Rosenberg went into his "I did not" testimony on the charges against him. His direct examination then proceeded as follows:

Q: *Did you ever have any conversation with Mrs. Ruth Greenglass about November, 1944, with respect to getting information from Dave Greenglass out of the place that he was working?*

A: I did not.

Q: *Did you know in the middle of November, 1944, where Dave Greenglass was stationed?*

A: I did not.

Q: *Did you know in the middle of November, 1944, that there was such a project known as the Los Alamos Project?*

A: I did not.

Q: *Did you ever give Ruth Greenglass $150, or any sum, for her to go out to visit her husband in New Mexico, for the purpose of trying to enlist him in espionage work?*

A: I did not.

Continuing in similar vein, Rosenberg denied that he ever had discussed espionage with the Greenglasses in Los Alamos. Referring to the fact that Greenglass, an Army technical sergeant, went home on furlough from Los Alamos in January, 1945, Mr. Bloch gave the witness the David Greenglass sketch of a cross-section of the Nagasaki atom bomb and asked:

Q: *I show you Government's Exhibit 2 and ask you whether or not Dave Greenglass ever delivered to you a sketch substantially similar to the sketch you hold in your hand, in January, 1945?*

A: He did not deliver such a sketch. I never saw this sketch before.

Q: *Did you know that he was working at Los Alamos Project?*

A: No, I did not know.

Q: *Did you associate in your own mind the words "secret project" with the Los Alamos Project?*

A: I did not.

Q: *Did you associate where Dave Greenglass was working in New Mexico with any project developing the atom bomb?*

A: I did not.

Q: *Did you, at any time during Dave Greenglass' furlough in New York in January, 1945, describe to him an atom bomb?*

A: I did not.

Q: *Could you describe an atom bomb today, or how an atom bomb works, or the component parts of an atom bomb and the functions of each part?*

A: Well, I heard in court a description of the atom bomb, and outside of that, I have never heard a description like that before, and I would say that I cannot repeat the description.

Q: *Did you ever take courses in nuclear physics?*

A: I did not.

Q: *Or any advanced physics?*

A: I did not.

Rosenberg added that he worker in the Emerson Radio Company doing research and development work on "some new projects they were making for the Navy and Army."

RED CONSPIRACY DESCRIBED

Earlier, Miss Bentley had told of the Communist conspiracy as the eighteenth prosecution witness. Appearing on the eleventh court day of the trial, she said her subpoena had interrupted her vacation in San Juan, Puerto Rico. She joined the Communist party in March, 1935. As an "underground worker" at Columbia University she said part of her work was "infiltrating the Teachers College newspaper there, so that we could influence its policies."

The American Communist party, she swore, was part of the Communist International in Moscow and subject to its orders. Disobedience by a party member meant expulsion, she said. After working with the late Jacob Golos, who died in 1943, she said she worked with Anitol Gromov, first secretary of the Russian Embassy. Spy information was then channeled through the Soviet Embassy in Washington, she said.

"The bulk of the work was collecting information from Communists employed in the United States Government and passing it on to Mr. Golos or other Communist superiors for transmission to Moscow," she said. "The Communist party being part of the Communist International only served the interests of Moscow, whether it be propaganda or espionage, or sabotage."

Miss Bentley said she had about thirty "contacts," including a telephone contact who identified himself as "Julius." Once, she said, she went to Knickerbocker Village with Golos and saw him meet a man who gave him written information late in 1942. This date preceded the period covered in the indictment by about two years.

When the defense objected, Judge Kaufman said the jury must decide whether the telephone Julius was in fact Julius Rosenberg. Miss Bentley said Julius lived in Knickerbocker Village, in reply to Mr. Saypol's questions.

On cross-examination, Emanuel Bloch made Miss Bentley admit that she lived with Golos outside marriage. When the lawyer asked if she were Golos' "mistress," she replied that she did not feel called upon to characterize the relationship. Mr. Bloch established that she now received money for lectures and a forthcoming book.

The defense attorney also brought out that Miss Bentley never had been arrested or indicted for Soviet espionage, though she had confessed her part in it to the Federal Bureau of Investigation in New Haven in 1945.

Since that time, she testified, she has given information on Communist activity to various committees of Congress and to lecture groups. Her book, she admitted, contained accounts of her telephone conversations with "Julius."

Mr. Saypol read to the jury from Sobell's draft board questionnaire, saying he had left blank an entry on possible prior military service. In 1943, Mr. Saypol established, Sobell's classification was first 2-A, a deferment from active duty because he was engaged in war work, presumably for the United States. Later, the Government prosecutor added, this 2-A classification was changed to Class 4-A.

Judge Kaufman adjourned the trial at 4:30 o'clock until 10:30 this morning, when Rosenberg's, direct examination will continue.

Story of the Rosenbergs: Two Links in Atomic Conspiracy

BY A. H. RASKIN | JUNE 21, 1953

THE EXECUTION OF JULIUS and Ethel Rosenberg on Friday night brought to an end a case that has stirred more worldwide interest than any American judicial proceeding since the Sacco-Vanzetti trial a quarter of a century ago. The Rosenbergs were sentenced to death for a new kind of crime in a new age — the age of atomic destruction. What follows is a narrative of the Rosenbergs' story as it was developed at their trial.

THE EARLY LIFE

The depression brought Julius and Ethel Rosenberg to communism, and communism brought them to one another. Born on Manhattan's poverty-ridden East Side, they embraced the Communist movement in their 'teens while millions of Americans were out of work and Franklin D. Roosevelt was struggling to put a splintered economy back into one piece.

Julius was a skinny, sallow youth, whose parents hoped he would become a rabbi but who found the faith of his fathers less satisfying than the faith that took its inspiration from the Kremlin. Ethel, two years his senior, was a plain-faced girl, petite without being pretty. They met while both were students at Seward Park High School. She got a job as a stenographer after graduation; he went on to City College but became so engrossed in Communist activities that he "flunked out" in 1937. He resolved to give more attention to his classes, was reinstated at the college and won his degree in electrical engineering in February, 1939. A few months later Julius and Ethel were married.

He bounced from one engineering job to another until he got a civil service appointment as a junior engineer in the Army Signal Corps on Sept. 3, 1940. That was the period of the Hitler-Stalin pact, when the Communists in this country were doing everything they could to obstruct our preparedness program, but there was no testimony that reflected adversely on Julius Rosenberg's performance of his job.

BEGINNING OF THE PLOT

After Pearl Harbor, with the United States and Russia established as wartime allies, Julius began to brood over the reluctance of our Government to entrust all its military secrets to the Soviet Union. He decided that the Russians were entitled to know everything we knew and that it was his responsibility to help them get any information they could not get through established channels of military or diplomatic communications.

His first big opportunity to help the Russians came in August, 1944, when the Army assigned Ethel's brother, David Greenglass, to work on the atomic bomb at Los Alamos, N. M. It was a full year before the first bomb was dropped on Hiroshima, and everything about the project was shrouded in deepest secrecy. Even Greenglass had no idea of what he was working on. He had been drafted in April, 1943, and had spent most of his time before he came to Los Alamos at the Aberdeen Proving Ground in Maryland. He had been a machinist before he got into uniform, and he was put to work in a machine shop at Los Alamos. All he knew about the significance of his job was that everything about the project was highly classified.

NEWS FROM HIS WIFE

David's first inkling of what it all meant came from a surprising source — his wife, Ruth. She went out to visit him in November, 1944. It was their second wedding anniversary, but their talk was not of marital affairs. Ruth told David she had had dinner a few days before with the Rosenbergs in their Knickerbocker Village apartment.

The conversation ran along a startling line. The Rosenbergs disclosed that they had joined the Communist underground — they were shunning open association with the party's activities, staying away from its meetings and not buying The Daily Worker. The explanation, as Ruth relayed it to David, was that "Julius has finally gotten to the point where he is doing what he wanted to do all along, which was that he was giving information to the Soviet Union."

After Ruth had gulped down the notion that Julius was a Russian spy he dished up an even more formidable mouthful for her to swallow. He told her that her husband was working on the atomic bomb and he urged her to rush out to New Mexico and bring back facts about the bomb for transmission to the Russians. Ruth's first response was that she would not ask David to cooperate, but she changed her mind when the Rosenbergs insisted that he would want to help and that the least she could do was pass the request on. Julius gave her $150 to pay for her trip.

GREENGLASS' ROLE

David was no more enthusiastic about the proposal than Ruth had been when he first heard it. He was frightened and hostile to the idea, but Julius' influence was strong, even with a continent between them. The G. I. thought over Julius' argument that Russia was fighting side by side with the United States and was not getting data she ought to have. After a sleepless night, David told his wife he would supply the information Julius wanted about the physical layout at Los Alamos, the number of people working there and the names of the key scientists supervising the project.

Rosenberg had instructed Ruth not to make any notes. She memorized David's answers and carried them back to New York. In January David came home himself on a twenty-two day furlough. Julius asked him to turn over everything he knew about the bomb that might be of value to the Soviets. Working from memory, David made sketches of a high-explosive lens, for which he had made molds in his New Mexico machine shop. (The lens is a curve-shaped high explosive used to set off the chain reaction that detonates the bomb.)

Greenglass had taken his duties seriously. He was able to supplement his sketches with a mass of technical material about the bomb and how it worked. He had wandered all over the top-secret "tech area" at Los Alamos, listening avidly to everything he could hear and questioning people "without their knowing it" to get a clearer idea of what they were doing. Julius was jubilant when David delivered his information. He said the sketches were "very good," and he got out a portable typewriter so Ethel could type up the data on the workings of the bomb. It took twelve pages to get it all down.

CONTACT WITH RUSSIANS

What did Julius do with the material he got from David? According to the Greenglasses, he had microfilming equipment concealed in a hollowed-out section on the underside of a console table that had been given to him by the Russians. Whenever he had a message or microfilm to turn over, he would leave it in the alcove of a movie theatre. When a personal meeting seemed in order, he would leave a note in the alcove, then rendezvous with his contacts in little-frequented spots on Long Island. Greenglass testified that on his furlough visit to New York Rosenberg had arranged to have him meet a Russian, whose name David never learned, on First Avenue, between Forty-second and Fifty-seventh Streets.

When David went back to his post, he took Ruth with him. He also took $200 Julius had given him for his sketches, and plans for supplying still more information to Julius' Russian friends. The first plan had been for Ruth and a woman named Anne Sidorovitch to exchange handbags in a Denver movie house, but this plan was scrapped in favor of a more ingenious one Julius thought up. He gave Greenglass an irregularly cut section of a Jello package and told him to have his information ready for transmission to a courier who would present the matching part of the package as identification.

DEALING WITH HARRY GOLD

The courier was Harry Gold, a Swiss-born biochemist, who had been a member of the Communist spy ring since 1935. He had no direct dealings with Rosenberg and he never made his identity known to Greenglass. Gold's contact was Anatoli A. Yakovlev, Soviet Vice Consul in

New York. He ordered the courier to undertake a double-barreled mission to New Mexico at the beginning of June, 1945.

One part of Gold's task was to go to Santa Fe and get data from Dr. Klaus Fuchs, a high-ranking British atomic scientist, from whom Gold had obtained vital material before. The other part was to visit Greenglass in Albuquerque. Gold objected that the trip to Greenglass might jeopardize what seemed to him the much more important job of contacting Fuchs, but Yakovlev insisted that he do both. At a meeting in a restaurant at Forty-second Street and Third Avenue, the Soviet diplomat gave Gold a note with Greenglass' name and address and the recognition signal, "I come from Julius." Along with the note went the companion half of the Jello panel Rosenberg had cut out for David.

In Albuquerque, on the morning of June 3, Gold went through the prescribed ritual of recognition signal and panel presentation. Greenglass walked across the parlor and fished the matching section out of his wife's pocketbook. The pudgy-faced courier sat down and introduced himself as "Dave from Pittsburgh."

PAID $500

Before departing with a fresh set of drawings and explanatory material from Greenglass, Gold gave the G.I. an envelope containing $500. The money came from Yakovlev. Two days later, Gold met the Russian on Metropolitan Avenue in Brooklyn and handed him two manila folders. One marked "doctor" contained the information the spy had got from Fuchs; the second marked "other" contained the Greenglass offering. Two weeks later Yakovlev told Gold that the material had been sent to the Soviet Union right away and that the data from Greenglass had proved "extremely excellent and very valuable."

RUSSIAN AS CO-CONSPIRATOR

The indictment that led to the Rosenbergs' death named Yakovlev as a co-conspirator, but he never came to trial. He left the United States on Dec. 27, 1946, and vanished behind the Iron Curtain.

Ethel and Julius Rosenberg, separated by heavy wire screen as they leave court after being found guilty by jury, 1951.

Rosenberg did not confine his professional interest to atomic information, according to the evidence at his trial. He confided to Greenglass that he had stolen the proximity fuse while he was working at the Emerson Radio Company on a Signal Corps project. He simply slipped the fuse into the brief case in which he had brought his lunch, and gave it to the Russians. His Communist ties cost him his civilian job with the Signal Corps on Feb. 9, 1945, even though he protested to his commanding officer that he had never belonged to the party. But neither his dismissal nor the end of the war brought a close to his career as a spy. In 1947 he told David about a fantastic "sky platform" that might be used as a launching site for guided missiles. He was well ahead of the public in learning that American scientists had solved the mathematical problems involved in the use of atomic energy for planes.

In June, 1948, he urged a City College classmate, Max Elitcher, not to give up a job as an electrical engineer in the Navy Bureau of Ordnance in Washington because the spy network needed a contact in the Navy Department. Elitcher spurned his advice. A month later, Elitcher was with another classmate, Morton Sobell, an electronics and radar expert, who worked on the classified Government contracts, when Sobell drove to Rosenberg's home with a 35mm film can filled with secret information. Tried with the Rosenbergs, Sobell drew a thirty-year jail sentence.

END OF THE ROAD

Rosenberg knew that the end of the road was in sight for him when the British announced the arrest of Klaus Fuchs in February, 1950. He warned Greenglass that Gold would be taken into custody soon and he recommended that David leave the country before he found himself behind bars, too.

When the F. B. I. jailed Gold on May 23 of that year, Rosenberg went into high gear. He gave Greenglass $1,000 and promised that the Russians would supply as much more as was needed to get David, his wife and their two small children out of the United States. The escape had been planned in elaborate detail. The family was to slip into Mexico on a tourist card; David was to send a letter to the Soviet ambassador's secretary, signing himself "I. Jackson" and saying something complimentary about the Russian position in the United Nations; then he was to take up a stance at a specified time beside a statue of Columbus, in Mexico City. He was to have a finger in a guidebook and, when a man approached, he was to say: "That is a magnificent statue. I am from Oklahoma, and I never saw anything like it." To which the man was to reply: "There are much more beautiful statues in Paris." Then the man was to give David money and passports that would carry the Greenglasses to an eventual haven in Czechoslovakia.

PREPARATIONS FOR FLIGHT

The thought of fleeing with a two-week-old infant did not appeal to

David and Ruth, but they pretended to fall in with the plan. Rosenberg gave them another $4,000, wrapped in brown paper. They later used the money to pay for David's lawyer at the spy trial. In the meantime, the Rosenbergs were making preparations of their own to get out of the country. They had passport pictures taken, but they were still here when Julius was arrested on July 17, 1950. Ethel was arrested less than a month later.

The only one who did leave after Fuchs and Gold had been apprehended was Sobell. He flew to Mexico City on June 21 with his wife and two children, leaving a brand new automobile in the garage of his Flushing home and giving no notice to his employer. He was deported from Mexico at the request of Federal authorities and arrested as he crossed the border at Laredo, Tex.

THE AFTERMATH

The Government has indicated that the death of the Rosenbergs will not end the story of their espionage. William Perl, one of America's foremost experts on jet propulsion, has been sentenced to a five-year prison term for falsely swearing that he did not know Rosenberg or Sobell, and the Justice Department says it is now in a position to link Perl to the spy network.

The Rosenbergs steadfastly denied throughout their trial that they had anything to do with espionage. They denied everything the Greenglasses and Gold swore to — meetings, money, microfilm, knowledge about the atomic bomb. They refused to answer questions about membership in the Communist party or the Young Communist League on grounds of possible self-incrimination, but swore that they were loyal to the United States.

CASE OF THE DEFENSE

The defense sought to convince the jury that David Greenglass had perjured himself in a deliberate effort to save his wife at the expense of his sister. Efforts also were made to get across the idea that Greenglass was personally unstable and unreliable, that he had been coached by the F. B. I., and that he had a grudge against Julius Rosenberg because of a business row they had when they were partners in a New York machine shop after the war. Greenglass, now serving a fifteen-year sentence for his part in the conspiracy, has assured his mother and elder brother that all his testimony was the truth and that he could not have shielded his sister without lying. Ruth Greenglass was not indicted for her part in the plot.

The echoes of the case will be heard as long as the "cold war" goes on. The legal point that split the Supreme Court will be tortured by a million amateur experts. The evidence that brought the jury's verdict and the judge's sentence will be lost in endless clouds of emotion, much of it politically generated.

British Tell How They Learned Nazi Secrets

BY THE NEW YORK TIMES | NOV. 10, 1974

ONE SUNNY MORNING in 1940, Col. Steward Menzies of Britain's Secret Intelligence Service sent four slips of paper to the British Air Ministry. Their contents were prosaic — routine personnel changes in the German Luftwaffe.

But they had been sent from one German commander to another and represented an extraordinary intelligence achievement. The intelligence service had proved that it could intercept high-level Nazi military signals and break the ciphers in which they were sent.

For five and a half years, Ultra, as the operation was called, provided British and United States leaders with the contents of secret messages between the top military and political leaders of the Third Reich.

At the most important periods of the war, Western leaders were able to learn the precise composition, strength and location of enemy forces and equally important, to determine what the enemy intended to do in many operations.

ULTRA OF 'PRICELESS VALUE'

Gen. Dwight D. Eisenhower said the Ultra intelligence was "of priceless value" and had saved "thousands of British and American lives. Winston Churchill termed Ultra, as it was called because it was ultrasecret, "my most secret source."

As the war spread across continents and oceans, Ultra reported to London and Washington the inner workings of the Axis military machine.

For a third of a century Ultra remained a secret. An official British ban on any mention of the operation was lifted last spring, This enabled a retired group captain of the Royal Air Force, Fred W. Winterbotham, formerly of the Secret Intelligence Service, to write the story of the operation in which he had played a major role.

His book, "The Ultra Secret," was published in London this fall by Weidenfeld & Nicholson. A number of American publishers are reported to be bidding for it because of its vivid picture of the manner in which intelligence of the highest sensitivity is gathered, processed and used in war.

The book adds a new dimension to the history of World War II.

Ultra intercepts of signals between Hitler and Gen. Günther von Kluge led to the destruction of a large part of the German forces in Normandy in 1944 after the Allied landing. Ultra enabled American fliers to shoot down Adm. Isoroku Yamamoto, the Japanese commander in the Pacific.

Why was Gen. George S. Patton, commander of the United States 3d Army, able to cross the Rhine in boats without artillery and air preparation? Ultra told him there was little opposition on the eastern bank.

Why was Adm. Chester W. Nimitz, the Pacific naval commander, able to escape a Japanese naval trap at Midway? Because Ultra told of Japanese intentions three weeks before they moved.

Ultra's usefulness had been extended to the Pacific war because the Germans had sold the machine to the Japanese.

Ultra's development is a story as bizarre as anything in spy fiction. It began in 1938 in a factory in eastern Germany where a young Polish mechanic was engaged in the manufacture of what he judged was some form of secret signaling machine. The Gestapo discovered his Polish nationality and deported him to Poland. He got in touch there with British intelligence.

The British smuggled him to Paris. There he was given a workshop and, with the aid of a carpenter, began to build a wooden mock-up of the machine he had seen in Germany.

Shortly it became apparent that the machine was an improved mechanical cipher machine called Enigma by its German makers.

The scene shifted back to Warsaw. There the British and Poles devised a plan to obtain a complete Enigma then being produced by the thousands to carry the secret signal traffic of the Nazi war machine.

Enigma was a system of electrically connected revolving drums around which ran the letters of the alphabet. A typewriter fed the letters of a message into the machine where they were so proliferated by the drums that, it was estimated, a team of mathematicians might require a month to work out all the permutations necessary to find the right answer for a single cipher setting.

INFORMATION USED CAREFULLY

In Britain, "backroom boys" — mathematicians from the great universities — set to work to duplicate Enigma. Using the then very new science of electronics they conquered the problems of Enigma variations and by late winter the British had a reproduction of the enciphering machine and the means of cracking the ciphers.

Then came the task of obtaining a single and correct translation of the signals that were deciphered in the original German.

The author says nothing about the means by which the signals were deciphered.

The problem arose of how the literally priceless information was to be passed on to the military. Obviously, if the Germans suspected a leak they would stop using Enigma, or make its operations even more complex.

Very strict rules were established to restrict the number of people who knew about the existence of Ultra information and to insure that no actions would alert the Germans that the Allies had knowledge of their plans.

Throughout the war at sea and in the air, these precautions were strictly observed. Ultra, for example, informed the British Navy in the Mediterranean of a sweep by the Italian fleet in 1941. The secret source of the information was protected by sending a flying boat ostensibly to "spot" the Italian fleet.

The Italians changed their plans. Ultra reported the change and the British caught them off Greece and crippled the fleet.

Ultra was the cause of one of Churchill's most agonizing decisions.

Luftwaffe orders used code-names for British cities during the bombing in 1940. But on the afternoon of Nov. 15 someone in Berlin slipped and the name Coventry came through Ultra. It would be four or five hours before the bombers reached the Midlands city.

Churchill had time if he chose, to order the evacuation of the population. But this would have been impossible to conceal, and evacuation would have given away the possession of prior information.

The Prime Minister took the tough course; he alerted the air force, the fire and ambulance services and the police. But the Germans blew the heart out of Coventry.

Californian Is Given 40 Years for Spying

BY ROBERT LINDSEY | SEPT. 13, 1977

LOS ANGELES, SEPT. 12 — Christopher John Boyce, a 24-year-old Californian who contended that he had been blackmailed into becoming a spy for the Soviet Union by a childhood friend, was sentenced to 40 years in prison today.

Federal District Judge Robert Kelleher said that he believed part but not all of Mr. Boyce's story that Andrew Dalton Lee, his one-time friend, had coerced Mr. Boyce into spying. The judge emphasized that whatever Mr. Boyce's motives, he felt that conviction of espionage was a charge that required a long prison term.

"There is a need for the word to go forth that to do the things that he and his co-defendant did will not be tolerated," Judge Kelleher said.

Mr. Lee was earlier sentenced to life imprisonment. Under Federal prison policy, it would be possible for Mr. Boyce to be released from prison after serving 14 years.

PROSECUTOR SOUGHT LIFE

Richard Stilz, an Assistant United States Attorney who had helped prosecute the case, had asked for life imprisonment for Mr. Boyce. Mr. Stilz charged that Mr. Boyce had "betrayed" his country and that information he gave to the Soviet Union had caused a grievous danger to the United States.

Until last December, Mr. Boyce worked in a secret code room operated for the Central Intelligence Agency by TRW Systems Group in suburban Redondo Beach near here. The Government had charged that Mr. Boyce passed along secrets to Soviet agents for almost two years, using Mr. Lee as a courier on monthly trips to the Soviet Embassy in Mexico City.

Among other things, the Soviet Union is believed to have been given vast amounts of data about a secret "spy in the sky satellites" built by TRW and satellites that monitor the Soviet Union and China for ballistic missile launchings.

Mr. Stilz said that only a portion of the material passed along to the Soviet agents became known at the trials of the two men. Documents sold to the Russians, he asserted, "were so extremely sensitive that our Government did not dare expose them at trial."

Judge Kelleher admitted to a dilemma in deciding on sentence. Looking down at Mr. Boyce, he said: "I think this defendant was corrupted by an evil person. I think this defendant has within him some decency and some real potential for that decency to be manifested and be useful to society."

At the same time, the judge said he believed that much of the defendant's story of coercion had been made "of whole cloth."

In an interview 10 days ago at the Terminal Island Federal Prison near here, Mr. Boyce had expressed remorse for his participation in the espionage operation and said he hoped some day to return to college and study to become a lawyer. At that time, Mr. Boyce had hoped his sentence might be as light as six years.

BLACKMAIL AND FEAR

Occasionally approaching tears as he described what he said was a two-year ordeal of blackmail and fear, he said he found himself in a trap from which he knew no way of escaping. "I was just as afraid of the F.B.I. and the Central Intelligence Agency as I was of the K.G.B. and Lee crime contacts. It was just a hopeless situation," he asserted. The K.G.B. is the Russian secret police.

Mr. Boyce said that when he went to work at TRW he had no idea that he would actually be working for the C.I.A. "I'm very sorry I ever had anything to do with the Central Intelligence Agency," he said.

Originally, Mr. Boyce said, he gave Mr. Lee secret data that, Mr. Boyce said, showed the C.I.A. was secretly "manipulating the leadership" of Australian labor unions. Mr. Boyce said his anger at such tactics caused him to give the information to Mr. Lee to pass along to the public, but instead Mr. Lee sold it to the Russians and embroiled him in the operation. Asked about his reasoning behind the move, he tried to explain how his outlook on life had been formed. "My father is very moralistic, a solid conservative, and I was educated in parochial schools and always had a very moral outlook," he said. "Through high school, and after school, I just began to feel that I was let down by my Government.

A 'MEANS OF ESCAPE'

"When the time came when pressure was put on me, I didn't have all the resolve that I should," he continued. "In the back of my mind was the thought, what the hell was my country worth struggling for?"

Asked why he had kept more than $15,000 given him by the Russians, he said: "I didn't take any money until this had been going on for a year. The money was left at my house by Lee; eventually the Russians gave money directly to me once in Mexico City."

"The situation was so black and so hopeless it was like my only solace, it was another means of escape," Mr. Boyce said. "I spent the money to escape what was going on in my life. I got rid of it as fast as I could because it was evidence of something that was evil."

"I spent it drinking, on parties, flying out of town on weekends, getting away from everything; it's very easy to spend money fast," Mr. Boyce said.

A Cryptic Ploy in Cryptography

EDITORIAL | BY THE NEW YORK TIMES | OCT. 29, 1977

THERE ARE MOMENTS when a scientific development becomes too important to be left to scientists alone. When uranium fission was discovered, Leo Szilard tried unsuccessfully to get Western researchers to stop publishing; it took government action to keep research secret until after Hiroshima and Nagasaki. The same point was reached in molecular biology a few years ago when techniques for manipulating recombinant DNA — gene splicing — were developed. This produced the self-questioning that led to voluntary restraints, Federal guidelines and legislation pending before Congress. Now, some argue, the same critical point has been reached in the branch of applied mathematics that studies cryptography.

Researchers at Stanford and M.I.T. have worked out ways to invent apparently unbreakable coding systems. There is evidence that this greatly concerns the National Security Agency — the ultra-secret Government organization whose job it is to decode foreign communications. N.S.A. evidently has tried informally to impede the university research, going so far, some say, as to raise the question of why it is being financed by the Government.

It is understandable that N.S.A. may be disturbed. Many successes in World War II reflected the Allies' ability to break German and Japanese codes. Unbreakable codes raise the prospect of the Soviet Union, for example, being able to communicate with perfect security in peace and war.

The researchers view the matter differently. A key figure, Dr. Martin E. Hellman of Stanford, argues that with modern computers it is relatively easy to work out unbreakable codes and N.S.A.'s code-breaking functions are doomed whether or not he and others publish their findings. By reporting on their research, Dr. Hellman argues, the investigators have opened the way to genuine privacy of communications at home as well as abroad at a time when society is depending increasingly on electronic communication.

The dispute may be moot. Enough about the code research has already been published to give an excellent picture of what the American scholars have devised. Yet it is disturbing that one major American university library is said to have removed from its shelves the published reports that touched off the controversy. This entire matter deserves to be examined by the larger community. Is Dr. Hellman right? Are computer codes headed rapidly toward invincibility regardless of what he and his fellow researchers have done? If so, what conceivable harm can the published research do? If not, why is N.S.A. not openly proclaiming the danger and arguing for a proper policy response? So far, the Government's responses have been, alas, cryptic.

CHAPTER 4

1980–1999: Dawn of the Computer Age

As the Cold War wound down and fears of atomic war lessened, the country welcomed the upsurge in technology generated by the space race against Russia. The commercialization of computers offered new possibilities in cryptography, efforts that both interested and concerned the U.S. government. The use of the internet for shopping and cellular phones for portable communications raised new challenges for privacy.

Science Agency Blocks Funds to Aid Research on Computer Coding

BY JOHN NOBLE WILFORD | AUG. 27, 1980

THE NATIONAL SCIENCE FOUNDATION has agreed, in an arrangement with the National Security Agency, to withhold funds for part of an academic research project in cryptography in a move that scientists fear is a step toward giving the secret intelligence agency control over advanced computer encoding research, whether military or civilian.

The intelligence agency said that it wanted to finance the project, and probably other such efforts, because of the national security implications of making and breaking codes. Many scientists viewed this latest development in the long-simmering conflict between the agency and the scientific community as a potential infringement of academic freedom.

QUESTION OF COMPUTER PRIVACY

In more practical terms, concerned scientists contend, the action raises the specter of military and intelligence intrusion in the increasingly sensitive matter of how to protect individual privacy and private business secrets, given the growing use of computers for such data.

If independent cryptographic research is not supported and its results disseminated, these scientists contend, it will be hard to keep medical, tax, banking and other private information private and safe.

The issue flared in scientific circles two weeks ago, when Leonard Adleman, a computer scientist at the Massachusetts Institute of Technology and the University of Southern California, learned that the National Science Foundation had passed his research proposal on to the National Security Agency, which then approached him with a promise of eventually providing funds. The issue received wider attention through a report in this week's issue of the journal Science.

Dr. Adleman said in an interview yesterday that he was reluctant to work under the aegis of the agency if it meant that the results would be classified as secret and never made available to the public.

Both Dr. Adleman and Ronald Rivest of M.I.T. are working on one of the most fundamental questions of computer mathematics: What makes computation problems easy or difficult almost to the brink of impossibility? Answers would help in developing codes that were harder and harder to crack.

Dr. Rivest's research is also being considered for support by the security agency. He said in an interview today that he would feel "more comfortable" working with the science foundation and that besides, M.I.T. had a policy against allowing faculty members to do classified research on the campus.

Vice Adm. Bobby Inman, director of the security agency, said in an interview that he understood the "instinctive objections" of many scientists to working for an intelligence operation and that he was attempting to develop a "dialogue" to reach some acceptable arrangements.

'OUR PEOPLE GOT NERVOUS'

The National Security Agency has primary responsibility for the collection of intelligence information through the electronic monitoring of ground and satellite communications throughout the world. Until a few years ago, it and other intelligence and military organizations had a virtual monopoly on cryptographic research.

Three years ago, Admiral Inman said, "our people got nervous about all the new work going on in the academic world." This was when the agency first sought to suppress some developments and to consider commissioning outside projects.

The National Science Foundation is the Government's primary conduit for financing basic research and is virtually the only source of support for basic studies in mathematics such as those involved in cryptography. A foundation spokesman said the situation was "complex," involving the foundation's responsibilities to science and to the "real needs" of national security.

Admiral Inman said that he had reached an agreement with Richard Atkinson, who until recently was the science foundation director, for the foundation to send all of its cryptography proposals routinely to the security agency for scientific review with an eye to possible support by the agency. The recent proposals by Dr. Adleman and Dr. Rivest were the first to attract the security agency's serious interest.

As the admiral explained it, the agency's plan is to provide grants for promising research by outside scientists, let them pursue the work as they ordinarily would and then have them present their results for review before publication.

He said that experts other than agency members would participate in the review. Any aspects of the results that were deemed sensitive would be classified secret, but anything else could be published. The scientist could then choose whether he wanted to continue work that happened to be classified as secret or to bow out.

Dr. Adleman said that he and other scientists wanted "some show of good faith" before they would consider undertaking security agency projects, including a "moratorium" on attempts by the agency to obtain legislation giving it substantial control over all cryptographic research and an acknowledgment that highly secure codes are essential in the private sector.

Researchers to Permit Pre-publication Review by U.S.

BY RICHARD SEVERO | NOV. 1, 1980

A GROUP OF MATHEMATICIANS and computer scientists has tentatively decided to try to dispel a concern of the National Security Agency by voluntarily submitting research papers to the agency for review before they are published in the scientific literature.

The National Security Agency, which has the responsibility for collecting intelligence information, is concerned because, it says, cryptographic research in universities has become so advanced in recent years that it is viewed as a security hazard. Until a few years ago the Government had a virtual monopoly on such research.

Cryptography, the art of writing or deciphering messages in code, has increasingly become a focus of academic interest, in great measure because of the need to protect industrial secrets. There is said to be apprehension within the National Security Agency over whether an academic researcher might write a paper on methods of analytically attacking and breaking a code system similar to one used by the Government.

The decision to attempt to cooperate with the agency without violating the tradition of academic freedom was made at a recent meeting of the Public Cryptography Study Group. Details of the precise form the cooperation will take, beyond allowing agency review, have not been formulated.

CONCERN ABOUT POSSIBLE CONTROL

The group was set up last year by the American Council on Education, which is made up of university administrators. The study group itself is nine members representing professional societies in computer sciences and mathematics. It does not represent all cryptographers, and some remain acutely concerned that the cooperation may become the first phase of Federal control over cryptography in American universities.

Daniel Schwartz, general counsel of the agency, said yesterday that nothing of the sort was contemplated. Asked what the Government would do if the voluntary program did not work, Mr. Schwartz said the agency "would consider as one option seeking legislation if the problem became serious enough and there was no other way to resolve it."

But he emphasized the agency considered such an action a last resort and added: "We have no interest in going through an enormous fight in the Congress on this particular issue." He said the agency would probably not object to most papers and if it did, the problem might be resolved by the deletion of an explanatory footnote.

CONFLICT CONCERNING FINANCING

Dr. Ronald Rivest, a computer scientist at the Massachusetts Institute of Technology, said he thought the study group's recommendations might be workable. "But I think it is important not to forget that the need for any sort of recommendations has not been made to anybody's satisfaction outside of the National Security Agency," Dr. Rivest added.

He was asked how he would feel about the financing of his work by the agency. Agency financing of academic research has been a disputed issue in recent years.

"I feel it is institutionally inappropriate," he said. "There would be a conflict of principles within the National Security Agency. On the one hand it would be concerned with maintaining national security, and on the other hand it would be concerned with maintaining the principle of open and academic research."

Dr. Martin Hellman, professor of electrical engineering at Stanford University, said he was also ready to try to cooperate. "If it doesn't work," he said, "we can back off." Dr. Hellman said he thought the agency had become easier to work with in recent years.

The relationship between academic cryptographers and the agency became a matter of some controversy last August when Leonard

Adleman, a computer scientist at M.I.T. and at the University of Southern California, learned that the National Science Foundation had passed his research proposal along to the National Security Agency, which then approached him about the possibility of providing some funds.

Dr. Adleman said he wanted no money from the agency. Since then he has been allowed to re-apply for money from the National Science Foundation.

E.S. Friedman, 88, Cryptanalyst Who Broke Enemy Codes, Dies

OBITUARY | BY ALFRED E. CLARK | NOV. 3, 1980

ELIZEBETH SMITH FRIEDMAN, a cryptographer who helped decipher codes used by enemies of the United States in both World Wars and who aided in the solution of international drug and liquor smuggling cases, died Friday at Abbott Manor, a home for the elderly in Plainfield, N.J. She was 88 years old.

At various times, Mrs. Friedman was employed by the Treasury, the United States Army, the United States Navy and the International Monetary Fund. Her husband, Lieut. Col. William Friedman, who died in 1969, was head of the Army's Cryptanalysis Bureau, responsible for breaking the "Purple Code," which was used by Japanese diplomats before and during World War II.

Mrs. Friedman began her career in cryptography in 1916, at the 500-acre Riverbank estate of George Fabyan in Geneva, Ill. Mr. Fabyan, a textile merchant, had established a center for code analysis that was taken over by the Government in 1917 for a training school in military cryptography.

At the Fabyan Laboratory, she was involved in breaking codes used by enemies of the Allies in World War I. She also met her husband-to-be at the laboratory, where he was working in genetics research, and they spent their early married years there.

BROKE BOOTLEGGERS' CODE

After leaving Riverbank for Washington with her husband in 1921, Mrs. Friedman was an assistant cryptanalyst for the War Department in 1921-22 and a cryptanalyst for the Navy in 1923.

During Prohibition, she was called upon to break complex radio codes used by rum runners in offshore operations that had stymied law-enforcement agencies.

Elizebeth Smith Friedman.

The Canadian Government enlisted her help in 1937 to crack a complicated code used in opium-smuggling operations by a Chinese gang headed by Gordon Lim. She succeeded, although she knew no Chinese, and Mr. Lim and four others were convicted on her testimony.

Her code-breaking prowess proved crucial in solving the "Doll Woman Case" in 1944. The incident involved Velvalee Dickinson, a dealer of antique dolls in New York City who was convicted of spying for the Japanese Government.

Mrs. Friedman, the youngest of nine children of a wealthy dairyman, was born in Huntington, Ind. She attended Wooster College in Wooster, Ohio, and graduated from Hillsdale College in Hillsdale, Mich., where she majored in English. She was awarded an honorary doctor of laws degree by Hillsdale in 1938.

She and her husband wrote "The Shakespearean Ciphers Examined," disputing the argument that Sir Francis Bacon had written the sonnets and plays of William Shakespeare.

Mrs. Friedman spent her retirement years compiling a bibliography of her husband's work for presentation to the George C. Marshall Research Library in Lexington, Va.

She is survived by a son, John, of Plainfield, N.J.; a daughter, Barbara Atchison of Berkeley, Calif., and five grandchildren. A memorial service will be held Wednesday at 7 P.M. at the Cosmos Club in Washington. She is to be buried in Arlington National Cemetery, at her husband's gravesite.

F.B.I. Said to Have Sent Messages to Spy Suspect

BY PHILIP SHENON | AUG. 13, 1985

WASHINGTON, AUG. 12 — The Federal Bureau of Investigation sent coded messages more than a year ago to a man now described by prosecutors as a member of a Navy spy ring, proposing a meeting with him in Mexico, sources knowledgeable about the case said today.

Classified advertisements published in The Los Angeles Times last summer were addressed to "RUS." This is a code name that the bureau says was used by Jerry A. Whitworth, a retired Navy radioman charged with providing the Soviet Union with secret Navy documents.

Use of the advertisements, the sources said, had been recommended by RUS in a letter sent to the San Francisco F.B.I. office in which RUS offered to expose a "significant" spy ring. F.B.I. communications were placed in the "personal messages" column in the newspaper on Mondays last summer, the sources said.

'ABSOLUTELY NO EVIDENCE'

Mr. Whitworth has pleaded not guilty, and his lawyers have strenuously denied that he was "RUS" or was involved in what the Government says was a spy ring run by John A. Walker Jr., a retired Navy communications specialist who has been described as Mr. Whitworth's closest friend. Mr. Walker has also pleaded not guilty.

"There's absolutely no evidence to connect Jerry with RUS," said Jim Larson, one of the lawyers. "The Government's best efforts to try to establish a connection between the two failed, as best I know."

A Federal official said the F.B.I. had not found Mr. Whitworth's fingerprints on the typewritten letter, nor did the typeface of the letters match any typewriter or printer found in a search of his home in Davis, Calif., near Sacramento.

'CONSIDERING YOUR OFFER'

The authorities said they were able to establish RUS's identity because of documents found in Mr. Walker's home.

According to the bureau, RUS, who listed his address as "Somewhere, U.S.A.," said in two letters to the bureau that he was willing to expose a 20-year-old spying operation in exchange for immunity from prosecution.

An advertisement on May 21, 1984, said: "RUS: Considering your offer. Call weekdays 9am — 11am." It was signed "ME, SF," and contained a northern California telephone number.

In an advertisement on Aug. 13, the sources said, the F.B.I. proposed the Mexican meeting. "RUS," it began. "Haven't heard from you, still want to meet. Propose meeting in Ensenada, Mexico, a neutral site. If you need travel funds, will furnish same at your choice of location in Silicon Valley or anywhere else."

This message followed an advertisement on June 11, 1984, in which the F.B.I. recommended a meeting on a San Francisco street corner, near the bureau's office, the sources said.

"RUS: Considering your dilemma," the advertisement said. "Need to speak with you to see what I can do. This can be done anonymously. Just you and I at 10AM June 21st at intersection of the street of my office & Hyde St. in my city."

'NEWSPAPER IN MY LEFT HAND'

The 19-line message went on: "I'll carry a newspaper in my left hand. We will only discuss your situation to provide you with guidance as to where you stand. No action will be taken against you whatsoever at this meeting. Respond if you cannot make it or if you want to change locations I want to help you in your very trying situation but I need facts to be able to assist you."

The meetings in San Francisco and Mexico did not take place, according to a high-ranking law-enforcement official. "Nothing came of that," he said. "RUS decided it was a bad idea."

Mr. Walker's brother Arthur was convicted last week of espionage and faces life in prison. Michael L. Walker, John Walker's son, has also been charged in the case. He also has pleaded not guilty.

According to the Federal Bureau of Investigation, the first of the letters from RUS arrived at its San Francisco office on May 11, 1984.

"In this letter," according to an affidavit signed by John H. Peterson, a bureau agent, "RUS states that he has been involved in espionage for several years and that he has passed top secret cryptographic keylists for military communications and other intelligence information to his contact, who provided the information to agents of the U.S.S.R."

The letter, postmarked Sacramento, offered RUS's cooperation "in breaking up a 'significant espionage system' in return for 'complete immunity' and no disclosure of his identity," Mr. Peterson said.

The F.B.I. said it received a letter from RUS dated May 21, the day of the advertisement urging him to call the number in San Francisco.

The letter, according to Mr. Peterson's affidavit, "contained further discussion of the possibility of and desire for immunity in return for information concerning RUS's contact, who, according to RUS, has been involved for more than 20 years and plans to continue indefinitely." Law-enforcement officials have said the "contact" was John Walker.

But a letter from RUS dated Aug. 13, the day of the advertisement proposing the Mexico meeting, said he had decided "it would be best to give up on the idea of aiding in the termination of the espionage ring," the affidavit said. "No additional communications were forthcoming."

Coding Techniques Are Detailed at Navy Spy Trial

SPECIAL TO THE NEW YORK TIMES | MARCH 27, 1986

SAN FRANCISCO, MARCH 26 — Attorneys on both sides in the espionage trial of Jerry A. Whitworth continued today to struggle with the task of making the world of secret cryptography understandable to the jury within the strictures imposed for discussing classified work.

Prosecutors are using what looks like an innocuous gray metal box, actually a KW-7 cryptographic machine, to demonstrate the workings of similar machines to which Mr. Whitworth had access as a Navy radioman with a top-secret clearance.

The machines hold the circuit boards containing the logic by which messages are encoded. A key card is used to reprogram the logic daily in the cryptographic machine before a message can be scrambled and unscrambled at the receiving end.

Mr. Whitworth had access to such keying material as the custodian of highly secret documents kept under tight security in ship vaults.

Under cross-examination today by James Larson, a defense attorney, Earl D. Clark Jr., who worked as an expert in communications security for the National Security Agency until his retirement last month, acknowledged that a KW-7 had been captured by the North Koreans in 1968 when they seized the United States spy ship Pueblo.

Federal District Judge John P. Vukasin, Jr. denied a defense motion that Mr. Clark's testimony regarding the value of diagrams of the machines' logic contained in technical manuals be stricken from the record. The defense made the motion after Mr. Clark admitted he had no engineering or mathematical expertise regarding the logic used in cryptography.

Mr. Clark had testified that photographs of the diagrams could allow a foreign power to reconstruct the encoding logic. Such reconstruction from drawings has been done in National Security Agency laboratories, he said.

Mr. Clark acknowledged that the manuals containing the logic diagrams had only a confidential classification, rather than the more restrictive secret or top-secret classification, and therefore had a wide distribution.

The prosecution contends that logic diagrams were sold to Soviet agents as part of an espionage conspiracy headed by John A. Walker, Jr., who has pleaded guilty to charges that he spied for the Soviet Union. Mr. Whitworth is accused of passing encryption devices and key lists to Mr. Walker.

Mr. Whitworth, 46 years old, is charged with eight counts of espionage and five counts of filing false tax returns and conspiracy to defraud the Government. He has pleaded not guilty.

The keying material would not have allowed the Soviet Union to simultaneously decode the daily messages of the Navy's communications system because of the reprogramming every 24 hours. The Government alleges that Mr. Whitworth met Mr. Walker to pass on information about twice a year over a 10-year period beginning in 1974.

Because the prosecution is required to prove that Mr. Whitworth passed the materials knowing that they would be of benefit to the Soviet Union or harmful to the United States, they have sought to establish that even the old, used keying cards were of great value.

"A used key is the most critical information you can get," Mr. Clark testified. He said it would allow the Soviets to decode material already compiled through their spying efforts.

Master Chief Thomas F. Bennett, a Navy radioman with 25 years' experience, told the jury the used materials are of such importance that they were the first items to be destroyed should a ship be in danger of being captured.

He also testified that Mr. Whitworth had had an exemplary military career from the time he joined the Navy reserve as a teen-ager until he retired as a Chief Petty Officer in October 1983. "He did an outstanding job. I would have loved to have someone like that working for me," Chief Bennett said.

Master Chief William F. Linne, similarly testified that Mr. Walker's record gave no indication he could not be trusted with classified information. He said Mr. Walker was evaluated by the Navy as having a "exceptionally high level of performance" and as "predictably reliable."

Biggest Division a Giant Leap in Math

BY GINA KOLATA | JUNE 20, 1990

IN A MATHEMATICAL FEAT that seemed impossible a year ago, a group of several hundred researchers using about 1,000 computers has broken a 155-digit number down into three smaller numbers that cannot be further divided.

The number is about 50 digits longer than any that mathematicians have reported being able to break down in the same way, an unusually long leap in this area of mathematics.

The latest finding could be the first serious threat to systems used by banks and other organizations to encode secret data before transmission, cryptography experts said yesterday.

These systems are based on huge numbers that cannot be easily factored, or divided into numbers that cannot be divided further. For example, the factors of 10 are 2 and 5.

FIRST BREAK IN THE SYSTEM

This is the first time that mathematicians have factored a number of the size used in these coding systems, said Dr. Arjen Lenstra, director the project who is at Bellcore Inc., in Morristown, N.J., the research arm of the Bell operating companies.

To break the huge number into three smaller numbers, which are 7, 49 and 99 digits long, the mathematicians had to find a new method because the one used in recent years was not up to the job. If someone had asked him to break up a 155-digit number a year ago, Dr. Lenstra said, "I would have said it was impossible."

Dr. Andrew Odlyzko, a mathematician at the American Telephone and Telegraph Bell Laboratories in Murray Hill, N.J., said: "This is a great achievement. From the standpoint of computational number theory, it represents a breakthrough."

The number itself was famous among mathematicians as a factoring challenge. In October 1988, mathematicians reported the factoring of a 100-digit number. It is a rule of thumb in mathematics that for every 10-digit increase in the size of a number, the amount of computing needed to factor it increases 10 fold. Until now, factoring advances had come in increments of 10 digits or less.

SECRETS ARE AT STAKE

But the practical importance of the result, experts said, is what it might mean to cryptography. In 1977, a group of three mathematicians devised a way of making secret codes that involves scrambling messages according to a mathematical formula based on factoring. Now, such codes are used in banking, for secure telephone lines and by the Defense Department.

In this system, a string of letters in the message are replaced by a number. That number is multiplied by itself many times, making a bigger number that helps mask the message. Then the big number is divided by a large number whose factors are secret. The remainder of that division — the amount left over — is the coded message. It can only be decoded by a person who knows the secret factors of the large number.

In making these codes, engineers have to strike a delicate balance when they select the numbers used to scramble messages. If they choose a number that is easy to factor, the code can be broken. If they make the number much larger, and much harder to factor, it takes much longer for the calculations used to scramble a message.

For most applications outside the realm of national security, cryptographers have settled on numbers that are about 150 digits long, said Dr. Gus Simmons, a senior fellow at Sandia National Laboratories in Albuquerque, N.M., who advises the Defense Department on how to make coding secure.

BROADER APPLICATION SEEN

Dr. Lenstra, who also led in the breaking of the previous 100-digit number, said: "For the first time, we have gotten into the realm of what is being used in cryptography. It means it is impossible to guarantee security."

Although the number the group factored had a special mathematical structure, Dr. Lenstra and his colleagues say the factoring method can be modified so it would have broad application.

Others are more circumspect. Dr. Simmons said that although he agrees that the method is generally applicable, he is waiting to see whether it can break down other numbers quickly enough to be practical. The method, he said, "may become of concern to cryptographers, but that depends on how efficiently it can be implemented."

Nonetheless, Dr. Simmons said, he would not feel comfortable advising the use of a 150-digit number to maintain security. "If national security were hidden behind a 150-digit number, we're getting very close to a situation where it would be feasible to factor that," he said. "Do I advise the Government to use bigger numbers? You bet."

The newly factored number was the largest number on a list mathematicians keep of the 10 Most Wanted Numbers, which are large numbers that are set up as a challenge to factoring experts. And it is so large that it is inconceivable to even think of factoring it without special mathematical tricks.

ANSWER IN A FEW MONTHS

Dr. Mark Manasse of the Digital Equipment Corporation's Systems Research Center in Palo Alto, Calif., calculates that if a computer could perform a billion divisions a second, it would take 10 to the 60th years, or 10 with 59 zeros after it, to factor the number simply by trying out every smaller number that might divide into it easily. But with a newly discovered factoring method and with a world-wide collaborative effort, the number was cracked in a few months.

The new factoring method was discovered last year by John Pollard of Reading, England, and Dr. Hendrik Lenstra Jr. of the University of California at Berkeley, the brother of Dr. Arjen Lenstra. The two mathematicians found a shortcut to factoring numbers of a particular form that happened to fit the form of many large numbers that were purposely derived so as to be difficult to factor.

Then Dr. Manasse and Dr. Arjen Lenstra recruited computer scientists and mathematicians from around the world to help in the factoring effort. Each person who agreed to help got programs sent electronically to their computers and a piece of the problem to work on.

LIKE A JIGSAW PUZZLE

It was like solving a giant, and twisted, jigsaw puzzle, Dr. Manasse said. Each computer was set to work doing the mathematical equivalent of sorting through a box with about 50 million pieces "including all sorts of useless stuff that look like jigsaw pieces that are not," Dr. Manasse said, adding: "Each person has to find the real piecs in the box. Some boxes don't have any and some have just one or two."

After about a month, the researchers got back the equivalent of about two and a half million pieces of the puzzle. To speed up the search and the final putting together of the pieces that would allow them to factor the number, the researchers used a powerful computer at the University of Florida that finished the job for them in three hours.

The current factoring landmark is the latest in a series of what to mathematicians have been breathtaking feats. In 1971, mathematicians scored a coup by factoring a 40-digit number. Ten years ago, a 50-digit number was thought to be all but impossible to factor. Then, with advances in research that led to unexpected shortcuts, 60-, 70- and 80-digit numbers fell. A year and a half ago, the 100-digit number was cracked.

Tied Up in Knots, Cryptographers Test Their Limits

BY GINA KOLATA | OCT. 13, 1991

EDGAR ALLAN POE THOUGHT there was no such thing as an unbreakable code. "It may be roundly asserted that human ingenuity cannot concoct a cipher which human ingenuity cannot resolve," he wrote.

In this spirit, cryptographers have spent nearly 15 years picking at a code that the National Security Agency, the nation's code-making and code-breaking agency, helped design for business and government to use in banking and in transmitting sensitive, but unclassified, data over computer lines. Yet, to the surprise of many mathematicians and computer scientists, the code, known as the Data Encryption Standard, or D.E.S., has stubbornly resisted their efforts to penetrate it. Only recently has anyone found a dent in the code and that dent by no means breaks it. In fact, the new system is only a slight improvement over the laborious method of trying every possible key to the code until the correct one is chanced upon.

The encryption standard is "a Gordian knot," said David Kahn, author of "The Codebreakers" and "Seizing the Enigma."

Poking away at the code has become an unofficial hobby for many civilian cryptographers, whose frustrations have led them to ask, What is the N.S.A.'s secret in building codes? The N.S.A., whose initials, some say, stand for Never Say Anything, is not commenting, of course.

"N.S.A. sure knows a hell of a lot more than we do," said Dr. Cipher Deavours, the son of a cryptographer who is himself a cryptographer at Kean College in New Jersey and editor of Cryptologia, a journal for the field. "Whoever had his finger in designing the D.E.S. sure knew what he was doing," Dr. Deavours said.

Dr. Thomas A. Berson, a communications security expert in Palo Alto, Calif., agreed. "The fact that the D.E.S. has withstood attack from all quarters for so long shows it has amazing strength," he said. In fact, the slightest change in the code makes it easier to crack. "That demonstrates to me that there is theory about making codes that is not known to the outside world," he said.

To mathematicians and computer scientists, the encryption standard is a nagging challenge, a publicly available code that seems to thumb its nose at their attempts to crack it. These researchers believe that by exposing a weakness, they could protect those who rely on the code, warning them that others who are not so friendly might have discovered for themselves the Achilles heel and may already be reading their mail.

The D.E.S. takes a message, translated into the computer language of zeros and ones, and scrambles it by repeatedly applying mathematical operations. Like a lock with many possible combinations, the code has a family of many possible operations that can be used to scramble a message. Once one of these keys has been chosen, anyone who has it can encode or decode a message. To break the D.E.S., a spy would have to figure out the user's key.

The difficulty is that there are 2 to the 56th possible keys, which is about 72 thousand million million. A computer built especially to break the code could check all the keys in two hours, said Dr. Martin Hellman of Stanford University. But the machine would cost $10 million. For most people who wanted to decrypt unclassified data, an exhaustive search is likely to be too much trouble and expense. So mathematicians and computer scientists have been looking for shortcuts.

The recent attack on the D.E.S. was announced by Dr. Adi Shamir of the Weizman Institute in Israel, and his former student, Dr. Eli Biham. In a tantalizing message that they sent to friends through electronic mail, they claimed to have found a weakness in the code that makes breaking it slightly easier than trying every combination. The attack is still not practical because it requires nearly as many calculations as an exhaustive search. And it requires an encoded copy of a known message, meaning that a spy would have to somehow plant a message to be encrypted.

Dr. Shamir, in a telephone interview, said he will not reveal the details of his work until it is published in a few months. He said, however, that it is a refinement of a previously published method in which he was able to attack a simplified version of the D.E.S. by comparing unencrypted blocks of text with encrypted blocks and looking for patterns.

Dr. Shamir's reluctance led Whitfield Diffie, a cryptography expert at Sun Microsystems in Mountain View, Calif., to comment, "Adi is a master of the suspense campaign."

Not only did Dr. Shamir not break the D.E.S., but he found, in probing the code, that it is actually far stronger than anyone had imagined. In fact, Dr. Shamir said, it seems to be the strongest possible code of its kind. Dr. Shamir's method devastates similar codes. He and Dr. Bihan reported in a previous paper that they can use their methods to crack a competing family of codes that were proposed recently by the Japanese and that were on the verge of being accepted internationally.

WITHOUT A CLUE

What this means, said Dr. Deavours, is that "we do not have the slightest idea of what distinguishes a good code from a bad one." The Japanese codes, he said, "were claimed to be as secure as the D.E.S. and more appropriate for regular computers," because they did not require a special purpose chip for encoding and decoding. "Imagine the standards organization getting ready to accept this stuff and the next day cracking them turns out to be a footnote in Shamir's paper," he said.

Although reluctant to generalize, Dr. Berson agreed that "there's no theory for developing a cryptosystem." Except, apparently, within the N.S.A.

When they first began working on the D.E.S., mathematicians and computer scientists predicted an easy victory. Some argued that the N.S.A. would never have promulgated a code, to be widely used and sold, that it could not break. If an enemy used the code, the N.S.A. would want to read the enemy's messages. So some civilian cryptographers argued that the code must have a trap door — a secret way of breaking it. Once they found the trap door, they would be in.

Now many doubt that there is such a secret entry. "Not only did no one demonstrate a trap door, but no one has been able to show how you could even make one," Dr. Berson said.

Dr. Shamir agreed. "I would say that, contrary to what some people believe, there is no evidence of tampering with the D.E.S. so that its basic design was weakened."

Asked whether people who use the D.E.S. should be wary, Mr. Diffie said that a lot depends on how and why they use it. In banking, for example, people typically change the key every day. But a message that you hope will be secure for years, even if it falls into enemy hands, might be very vulnerable.

Mr. Diffie said that code breakers have been known to work for decades trying to decipher important messages. For example, in the 1930's, the British intelligence service got hold of an encrypted Soviet message thought to include the identities of spies. "They continued trying to read it for 30 years," Mr. Diffie said.

"If you are designing cryptosystems, you've got to think about long-term applications," he said. "You've got to try to figure out how to build something that is secure against technology in the next century that you cannot even imagine."

The Assault on 114,381,625,757,888, 867,669,235,779,976,146,612,010,218, 296,721,242,362,562,561,842,935,706, 935,245,733,897,830,597,123,563,958, 705,058,989,075,147,599,290,026, 879,543,541

BY GINA KOLATA | MARCH 22, 1994

MATHEMATICIANS SAY THEY are close to breaking a cryptographic stronghold that was not expected to fall for many years. The item is a 129-digit number that was first described in 1977 as proof of the security of a new public cryptographic system.

The number is known for short as RSA 129 after the initials of its inventors and its number of digits. The new coding system depended on very large numbers that were multiples of two primes, a prime being a number divisible only by itself and one.

The code could be cracked only by finding the component primes, one of the most mathematically difficult tasks imaginable. The inventors proposed RSA 129 as an example. Only they knew its component primes, and they asserted it would take others at least 40 quadrillion years to factor it, using the best methods and the fastest computers that were then available.

But over the years the number proposed as uncrackable simply became a challenge. Eight months ago, with the power of computers growing, cryptography enthusiasts proposed a cunning scheme to attack it. They would break the problem into millions of tiny pieces and then use volunteers recruited on the Internet, an international electronic mail system, to do the calculations on their computers, at night or in other fallow periods.

RSA 129 has not crumbled yet. But several factoring experts said that so many of the calculations have already been completed that they are confident the solution will emerge in a few weeks.

The inventors of RSA are Dr. Ronald Rivest, of the Massachusetts Institute of Technology, Dr. Adi Shamir of the Weizmann Institute of Science in Rehovoth, Israel, and Dr. Leonard Adleman of the University of Southern California.

The RSA code acts like a lockbox with two keys. One key is a large composite number, which the owner may distribute publicly. Anyone could use that key to open the box and put a message in for the owner. But once the message is put in, the lockbox can only be opened again by the owner, who has the second key, which is the two factors of the composite number. And only the owner knows those numbers, because he has purposely constructed the composite number from two large prime numbers.

Commercial cryptographic chips based on this scheme use numbers that are typically either 135 or 150 digits. But users can choose even larger numbers if they like. Dr. Rivest, who is also chairman of the company that makes the chips, says that even if the 129 digit number is cracked, their security will not be immediately threatened.

Dr. Arjen Lenstra, a factoring expert at Bellcore in Morristown, N.J., said the eventual factoring of RSA 129 was a near certainty. Dr. Andrew Odlysko, a factoring expert at A.T.&T. Bell Laboratories in Murray Hill, N.J., said although it was still possible that the effort to factor RSA 129 would fail, "It is extremely unlikely, probably much smaller than the chances of an asteroid hitting the earth tomorrow."

Dr. Odlysko said that putting together the pieces of the problem to yield the factors of RSA 129 was like turning over squares on "Wheel of Fortune." Just as, eventually, participants in the game show know that almost enough squares have been turned for the phrase to be guessed, so the mathematicians know that almost enough calculations have been completed so that discovery of the factors of RSA 129 is imminent.

The soon to be realized factoring of RSA 129 will be "a landmark," Dr. Odlysko said. "It shows us how far we can go," he added.

The attack on RSA 129 originated last summer, when Dr. Lenstra got a message from a group of Internet users who wanted help with a factoring challenge. The three computer hobbyists, Dr. Paul Leyland, who is a computer system manager at Oxford University in England, and two graduate students, Derek Atkins at the Massachusetts Institute of Technology and Michael Graff of Iowa State University, wanted to recruit volunteers to factor a large number, thinking of it as a sort of a mathematical game.

MAKING TASK 'REALLY INTERESTING'

"I told them, why don't you do something that's really interesting, like RSA 129," Dr. Lenstra said. They readily agreed.

The three advertised on an Internet bulletin board that is read by people interested in cryptography. So far, said Mr. Atkins, they have had 1,693 requests from volunteers for identification numbers, which are used to keep track of those working on the problem, and for pieces of the problem to work on. And, Mr. Atkins added, "every day more join in."

The Internet volunteers use computer programs supplied by Mr. Graff, Mr. Atkins and Dr. Leyland to do the calculations. Then they send their data to M.I.T., to be checked for accuracy. When all the data are in, Mr. Atkins will send them to Dr. Lenstra. He, in turn, will put them together in one immense calculation to yield the factors of RSA 129.

Factoring a number is one of the oldest and most difficult mathematical problems. It requires finding every prime number that divides into the number with no remainder. Factoring is simple for smallish numbers. The factors of 33, for example, are 3 and 11. The factors of 935 are 5, 11, and 17 because $5 \times 11 \times 17$ gives 935. But as numbers grow large, the task of testing every lesser prime to see if it is a factor quickly becomes very daunting.

For example, Dr. Lenstra said, to mount this kind of attack on RSA 129 would require testing 10 to the 50th, or more than one hundred thousand quadrillion quadrillion quadrillion primes. Using the conventional approach, this task could take up to a quadrillion quadrillion years. But, the code's designers said at the time, mathematical shortcuts might bring that down to 40 quadrillion years.

BASIS ON FACTORING SCHEME

No one has found a way to factor very large numbers with little effort, but mathematicians have taken nibbles at the problem. The method being used by the Internet volunteers is based on a factoring scheme invented in 1981 by Dr. Carl Pomerance of the University of Georgia, known as the quadratic sieve.

It allows a large and complex problem like factoring to be parceled out as millions of small pieces that, put together at the end, can yield a solution. Most of the pieces of data turn out to be useless to the final solution, but mathematical tricks allow the good data to be separated from the bad, like a sieve sifting gold nuggets from sand.

Even with the quadratic sieve, the factoring of RSA 129 will end up taking more than 10 to the 17th calculations. This is within a factor of a million of experts' best estimate of the total number of calculations ever done in the history of humanity, Dr. Adleman said. What made the effort work was the fact that computers have gotten so fast and that so many computers could be brought to bear on the problem.

RSA was a sensation when it appeared because it was entirely different from conventional cryptographic schemes, which use mathematical formulas to scramble data. Because there is no way to prove that their method is unbreakable, the cryptographers can only say that they asked experts to try to break it and none succeeded.

With RSA, in contrast, the only way to break the code is to factor a very large number that was used to scramble data. So the inventors could say that breaking the code was provably hard — it was as hard as factoring a particular large number.

SECURITY VS. SPEED

In theory, owners could use numbers as large as they want for encoding. But the larger the number, the longer it takes to encode data, so users have to balance their need for security with their need for speed. Dr. Rivest said the code is widely used by companies, and that more than three million copies of its software have been sold.

Dr. Adleman said he was happy to see the attack on RSA 129. "I congratulate them," he said. "It's a stimulating thing." Dr. Adleman himself contributed to the effort, joining the Internet volunteers.

Dr. Rivest said the effort to crack RSA 129 was "a demonstration of the difficulty of the problem." After all, Dr. Rivest said, RSA 129 "has been around for 17 years and it has taken this long to get up the stage where you can attack it."

Dr. Adleman said the attack posed little threat to the RSA scheme in general because making the number to be factored just slightly bigger added immensely to the difficulty of factoring. "Improvements in computer technology always favor the cryptographer over the cryptanalyst," he said.

Dr. Odlysko said he agreed with Dr. Adleman, but he added that the attack on RSA 129 did reveal something about the security of the code. "The real significance of the factoring of RSA 129," he said, "is that the foreseeable future 17 years ago did not envision being able to factor a number of this size."

No one predicted that individual computers would be so fast, that thousands of computers would be hooked up on Internet or that such significant technical advances would be made in the mathematics of factoring.

Dr. Odlysko said that an attack like the one on RSA 129 would be easy for many corporations or the Federal Government. "There are plenty of corporations that have much more computing power than was used in this project," he said. For example, he said, Sun Microsystems or A.T.&T. easily can best the Internet volunteers in computing power.

Dr. Odlysko said he felt that for most purposes a 150-digit number "is moderately secure right now, but I wouldn't trust it." He added, "When people ask me what is the minimum I would feel comfortable with, I tell them it is 230 digits." A number that large, for the near future, cannot be cracked.

Why I Spied: Aldrich Ames

BY TIM WEINER | JULY 31, 1994

A traitor tells how greed led him to condemn a dozen double agents to death or prison.

RICK AMES, A LIFELONG EMPLOYEE of the Central Intelligence Agency, betrayed at least 12 of the best secret agents working for the United States from within the Soviet Union and the Soviet bloc during the 1980's. All were jailed and most were executed. "They died because this warped, murdering traitor wanted a bigger house and a Jaguar," says the Director of Central Intelligence, R. James Woolsey.

From 1975 to 1985, the C.I.A. promoted Aldrich Hazen Ames, an alcoholic underachiever going through a financially ruinous divorce from a fellow spy, to increasingly sensitive posts, unaware that he was thinking all the decade about selling the agency's deepest secrets to Moscow. For the next decade, it remained unaware that he was hand-delivering reams of top secret papers to the Soviets and talking his vodka-soaked heart out with his Communist case officers in annual all-nighters.

Now Ames has to face the brutal consequences.

In 1962, Ames joined the C.I.A., where his father worked as an analyst. After three years undercover in Turkey, he married a C.I.A. colleague and they spent the 70's in Washington and in New York, where he hobnobbed with Soviets assigned to the United Nations and began to think about a double life. The marriage fell apart. He went alone to Mexico City, where he worked from 1981 to 1983. There, he met Maria del Rosario Casas, a Colombian cultural attache working for the C.I.A., the woman who would become his second wife and who would be charged as his accomplice. Deemed mediocre by his superiors, he was nonetheless elevated to chief of the Soviet branch of the counterintelligence division. His job was recruiting and running foreign agents.

Aldrich Ames being led from the U.S. federal courthouse in Alexandria on Feb. 22.

In 1985, Rick Ames recruited himself. He sold a Soviet Embassy official the names of two K.G.B. officers secretly working for the F.B.I. in Washington. The price: $50,000. The next month, he volunteered the names of every Soviet intelligence official and military officer he knew was working for the United States, along with whatever else he knew about C.I.A. operations against Moscow. In September of that year, shortly after he and Rosario married, he received a wedding present from the K.G.B.: $2 million. He claims he was shocked; the money was far more than any other American spy is known to have received from the Soviets. But then the Soviets never had a spy like Rick Ames.

He continued spying for nearly nine years, first in Rome, where he served from 1986 to 1989, and then from inside the agency's headquarters in Langley, Va. From 1990 to 1994, he oversaw operations in Western Europe against the Soviets and their satellites, ran spies in Czechoslovakia and worked in the C.I.A.'s Counternarcotics Center, flying to meet his Russian handlers in Bogota and organizing efforts against the heroin trade in Moscow — all the while waltzing out of his offices with classified papers to sell.

The arrest of Rick and Rosario Ames this February played first as tragedy, then as farce.

The C.I.A. had known since early 1986 that there was a traitor within. Meanwhile, Ames was flunking lie detector tests, plunking down a half-million dollars in cash for a new house and idling in a new Jaguar at the agency's gatehouse. Woolsey concedes that "appropriate resources were not dedicated promptly in the Ames case." After the arrest, newspaper cartoonists skewered the agency mercilessly, depicting a mole in a trench coat working unnoticed and unworried in a secret warren. The C.I.A. has been admired, feared and criticized during its 47 years. Now it is being ridiculed by Congress and the public, and that is a dangerous thing. Woolsey says he must "change the culture of the C.I.A" so that it will not be "a fraternity ... wherein once you are initiated, you're considered a trusted member for life."

Rick Ames now spends three days a week being grilled by F.B.I. and C.I.A. officers. He says the sessions are going fine; his interrogators are not sure he is telling them the whole truth. Hanging in the balance is the fate of Rosario Ames, who is to be sentenced Aug. 26. Her husband's cooperation may help her to get out of prison in a few years and be reunited with their 5-year-old son, Paul. But the spycatchers who spend their days in the labyrinth of Rick Ames's double life are nowhere near the end of their journey.

We began more than eight hours of one-on-one interviews on July 7 at the Alexandria, Va., city jail, Ames's temporary residence before he is transported to a maximum-security Federal prison for the rest of his life. Since the 53-year-old Ames was arrested, his hair and skin have grayed perceptibly. On the surface, he is smooth, beguiling, sometimes charming. He fumbles for words only when he considers the nature of his treason and then that calm exterior cracks. His interior? There is an emptiness where pain or rage or shame should be. Maybe that is the cost of a secret life. Maybe it was the alcohol; he was drunk for a good part of his three decades with the C.I.A. Maybe it is the fact that, in exchange for a fortune, he sold out a dozen men and condemned them to death or prison. He deals with this by saying he has sentenced himself to a living death too: "The men I sold. ... What happened to them also happened to me."

Q: *When you first signed up with the C.I.A. in 1962, what was it like?*

A: I felt proud and selected. They made a great effort, as do some units in the military, the Foreign Service, to cultivate a sense of being in the elite. Kids respond to that. Young men and women respond to that. And certainly I did. The ethics of espionage, of telling lies, cover stories, this didn't bother too many people. It didn't bother me. People saw it as part of the struggle. ... There was a sense of fun.

Q: *When did it stop being fun?*

A: I don't know that it ever stopped being fun, O.K.? I always thought it was fun. I don't think everyone else did, but I — yes. It was always fun. Turkey was wonderful. New York was probably the most fun I had. Mexico City was fun. And the job I had in '83 to '85 was the most fun headquarters job I had. It was really interesting. I mean, there were other things going on. My feeling that we had never done right by Soviet operations, never spent enough money, put enough people on it, took enough risks. But then that came together with a feeling of "well, wait a minute. Even if we did, would it be worthwhile?"

Q: *When did you make the decision to work for the other side?*

A: Some of that started in the 70's in New York.

Q: *Why?*

A: You know, I knew some Soviets in New York who were very interesting. The chief Pravda representative in New York and I had lunch together every couple of weeks for about three years. And he didn't directly teach me a lot, but indirectly I learned an awful lot … in terms of what the Soviets were all about. What happened later, frankly, is I got myself in the position where I thought, and still think — call it arrogance, if you will — but I'd say: "I know what's better. I know what's damaging and I know what's not damaging, and I know what the Soviet Union is really all about, and I know what's best for foreign policy and national security. … And I'm going to act on that."

Q: *What were your motives?*

A: Money — money was the — money was the motivation. These other ideas and reasons were only enablers, if you will. I mean, plenty of people need money. A number of people throughout the agency's history have stolen money from the agency and have done terrible things for money. Very few have sold secrets to the K.G.B., and I think one of the reasons is because many of them would have found — there were a lot of barriers in the way. For me, by 1985, some of those barriers weren't there any more. I don't believe that I was affecting the security of this country and the safety of its people. … I didn't give that stuff to the Soviets because I thought espionage is a dirty game. I mean, that's trivial.

Q: *How did you segregate the K.G.B. side of your life from the C.I.A. side?*

A: It's a normal human faculty. I adapted a little more in the sense of being able to deny things, to avoid thinking about consequences. I never spent a lot of time thinking about my relationship with the K.G.B. When I would meet them, when I would have personal meetings with the K.G.B. officers, say in Bogota, when I left that meeting, at maybe 2 A.M., having had the better part of a bottle of vodka also, but when I left that meeting, I would have made a few notes about the communications planned for the next year. When I left that meeting, I just filed it in the back of my mind. I never once sat back and said: "Now, let's see. What did we talk about?"

Q: *File it and forget it.*

A: File and forget. And I told the K.G.B. I worked that way, too. And it caused me problems. I mean, I would forget things. I would screw up meetings. And this is partly just pure negligence, but partly just — there was some mechanism operating that not only allowed me to do that but motivated me to do that in the first place. I didn't want to sit and mull it over.

Q: *Did drinking factor into any of this, as a means of forgetting?*

A: Yeah. The actual meetings I had with Soviets, for example, I would — I usually had several drinks before a meeting. I would drink during the meeting. They would try and keep it very paced and everything, and so I wouldn't be completely drunk, but I would definitely have had more than just enough to put an edge on. I have had a kind of on-again, off-again binge drinking problem that occasionally reached the edge of scandal, but never quite fell off.

Q: *You attacked espionage as a farce at your sentencing in April. What about the argument that the C.I.A.'s successes are all secret and only its failures are trumpeted?*

A: You know that fellow Tolkachev? [Adolf G. Tolkachev, a Soviet military official spying for the United States, was betrayed in 1985 — probably by Edward Lee Howard, a C.I.A. officer — and was executed in 1986.] Tolkachev provided an awful lot of very valuable information on Soviet avionics, and I heard people that described his contribution in terms of, "He pays the rent on the headquarters compound." The thought expressed was that what he was able to tell us meant that N.A.T.O. would have clear air superiority in the event of a Warsaw Pact invasion of Western Europe. Well, that certainly sounds like a spectacularly successful espionage operation, but then you've got to take a little reality check. No. 1, nobody in the U.S. military, in the Administration, in N.A.T.O. seriously believed that N.A.T.O. air superiority was ever in question anyway. That was not an issue. Reality check No. 2, the Warsaw Pact invasion of Western Europe? What's the percentage of that occurring? Vanishingly small. So when you put even some of the spectacular successes under scrutiny, you come up saying, "Do we need to be doing all this expense, all this risk, all the things associated with espionage — for this end?"

Q: *There's been quite a bit of debate inside and outside the C.I.A. — what's the agency's mission now that the cold war is over and the Soviets are gone?*

A: Everyone is pretending things haven't changed. And by God, the scales have to drop from our eyes at some point.

Q: *What would we see?*

A: We don't have a special mission. We have been … deluding ourselves politically and convincing ourselves that we have a special mission.

Q: *What do you think this delusion is?*

A: To connect the repression of however you want to describe movements for economic and social justice in this country with a hyped-up threat from abroad, and to try and link the two, and to attack both. I hate to sound like an old-line Stalinist or something, but. …

Q: *An enemy within?*

A: Right.

Q: *Someone once wrote that a nation can't be great without a great enemy.*

A: I suppose that's a condemnation of greatness. If you look at any great nation, it's inherently evil or acquisitive or aggressive. Greatness is based primarily on values that we abhor.

Q: *After '85, after you gave up the names of the Soviets working for the C.I.A. and went to the Rome station, how did you get information to pass to the K.G.B.?*

A: I just passed what I had access to. And I had access to a wide range of stuff, but not to Soviet, sensitive Soviet operations. Except little bits and pieces. But I had a wide range of other information that the K.G.B. was eager to get, and happy to get. Generally, operational stuff. In Rome — you would find it hard to believe, probably, I know the K.G.B. found it very hard to believe — that as much paper washes through our overseas stations as does. Every day, I would have a stack of paper like that [holds his hands a foot apart], from headquarters, from stations elsewhere in Europe and elsewhere around the world who for some reason thought to put Rome on the routing. Just tremendous volumes of stuff. Most of it rather trivial, but some of it was of interest. And so I passed a lot of that.

Q: *How would you arrange to contact the other side and meet?*

A: Through a go-between, a Soviet Embassy officer, who's not a K.G.B. officer. We had an overt relationship — I was assessing the guy to see if he'd be of value as a target and did develop him a little bit — so this was all approved. I would give him a bag with some magazines in it, and then with a couple of envelopes with documents. A stack about this high [holds hands six inches apart] in the bottom of it. And I'd give him that after lunch, and he would give me usually a box of Cuban cigars. I don't know where he got the idea I was a cigar smoker. They weren't really high quality. And that would contain some money. We never discussed the operation. He had a pretty clear idea of what was happening, about the kind of person I was, and we got very friendly. But we never talked about it. And then from time to time, a K.G.B. officer involved with the case would travel to Rome and we would have a meeting in the Soviet residential compound. We had a late-night meeting. I would be picked up in the car and they would drive around for about 40 minutes, making sure there was no surveillance. I would have a jacket and a baseball cap on, take my glasses off, hunch down and we'd go zooming in, and then they'd take me up to a little room they'd constructed up in the attic for me. And we'd sit there for about four or five hours. And then we'd zoom back out.

Q: *What were the immediate consequences of your acts?*

A: In '85, '86, as a result of the information I sold to the Soviets, it was as if neon lights and searchlights lit up all over the Kremlin, shone all the way across the Atlantic Ocean, saying, "There is a penetration." No reasonable counterintelligence officer, F.B.I. or the C.I.A., was under any doubt by the spring of '86 that a penetration of S/E [the C.I.A.'s Soviet-Eastern Europe operations division] was the single, most logical reason for the disasters that had occurred. ... It was almost inconceivable that the K.G.B. found itself doing what they did on the basis of the information I gave them. They went around and they wrapped all the agents up. I was amazed. I was anxious and amazed and shocked and scared. And in the course of the following years, all of the agents I told them about were recalled, transferred, arrested, whatnot, and then later on some of them were shot. ...

The scale of what I had given them, it just went too high, and the K.G.B. later told me that they regretted acutely that they had been forced to take those steps. Had I known they were going to do that, I either would not have gone and sold them that information or I would have passed them out one by one. Had the K.G.B. not handed the proof that there was a penetration on a silver platter to the world, would there have been a continuing effort over eight or nine years to keep on looking for the source of a problem? Good question.

Q: *Why do you think it took so long to catch you?*

A: You've got two or three or four thousand people running around doing espionage. You can't monitor it. You can't control it. You can't check it. And that's probably the biggest problem with an espionage service. It has to be small. The minute you get big, you get like the K.G.B., or you get like us.

Q: *Did you have any inkling that you were going to get busted?*

A: None. … I always found reasons not to engage in a serious sit-down and think, "Where have things come to?" Had I done that, I might have seen what was coming. I shrank from it, I guess. Because had I come to the conclusion, it would have meant taking steps, untakebackable steps.

Q: *You were scheduled to go to Moscow the week you were arrested. There was never any thought of, O.K., this is it, we're going to pull the plug and stay there?*

A: No, I hadn't thought that way and I wasn't planning to do that.

Q: *Getting out didn't cross your mind?*

A: No. Well, it crossed my mind, but it was never a serious plan.

Q: *A dozen people died or disappeared. People who, for whatever motives, — personal, psychological, financial, political — broke with their service to work for the United States. Deliberate acts of yours —*

A: Yes. Yes.

Q: *Led to their deaths.*

A: Yes.

Q: *Talk about that.*

A: It's really hard to talk to an outsider about it. It is hard to — there is a mystique, and it has nothing to do with facile things, like falling in love with an agent, but there is an old tradition in the agency — maybe it's still around. You get older, you tend to think it's faded by now. But I was a strong believer in the kind of bond — in addition to the overriding duties that you had as a case officer toward an agent, and your responsibilities to the agency and all that, you also had a kind of professional, personal, obligation. I think many, many people certainly felt that way, and probably still do. The process that enabled me to just suddenly — because it wasn't gradually — suddenly justify turning my back on the whole complex of what I just talked about, not to mention just the normal sense of human responsibility. ...

This — this — this has so many consequences, and is such a burden. There was a sense in which, perhaps — and it's hard for me to articulate it, or to fully understand it — in which I was saying: "Over to you, K.G.B. You guys take care of me now." You know, I have done this. I have demonstrated that I'm holding nothing back. You guys take care of me. There may have been a component like that. There also was a sense in which I was saying, "It will help protect me in the future if these guys go away." But it's not untrue to say that they took similar risks. That is a callous thing to say, but there is a certain amount of truth to that. These two guys in the K.G.B. residency in Washington, and lots of people elsewhere. You know, they took similar risks. So there's that reciprocity, if you will. I don't mean it to be taken in terms of dismissing the men I sold and trivializing that. In other words, what happened to them also happened to me. So.

Q: *Do you think it would have been better if you'd left the agency 10 years ago?*

A: Yeah. [Long pause.] My son would have his parents. [Long pause.] My wife would have a husband. [Long pause.] That's it.

TIM WEINER is a reporter in the Washington bureau of The New York Times.

Attention Shoppers: Internet Is Open

BY PETER H. LEWIS | AUG. 12, 1994

AT NOON YESTERDAY, Phil Brandenberger of Philadelphia went shopping for a compact audio disk, paid for it with his credit card and made history.

Moments later, the champagne corks were popping in a small two-story frame house in Nashua, N.H. There, a team of young cyberspace entrepreneurs celebrated what was apparently the first retail transaction on the Internet using a readily available version of powerful data encryption software designed to guarantee privacy.

Experts have long seen such iron-clad security as a necessary first step before commercial transactions can become common on the Internet, the global computer network.

From his work station in Philadelphia, Mr. Brandenburger logged onto the computer in Nashua, and used a secret code to send his Visa credit card number to pay $12.48, plus shipping costs, for the compact disk "Ten Summoners' Tales" by the rock musician Sting.

"Even if the N.S.A. was listening in, they couldn't get his credit card number," said Daniel M. Kohn, the 21-year-old chief executive of the Net Market Company of Nashua, N.H., a new venture that is the equivalent of a shopping mall in cyberspace. Mr. Kohn was referring to the National Security Agency, the arm of the Pentagon that develops and breaks the complex algorithms that are used to keep the most secret electronic secrets secret.

Even bigger organizations working on rival systems yesterday called the achievement by the tiny Net Market a welcome first step.

"It's really clear that most companies want the security prior to doing major commitments to significant electronic commerce on the Internet," said Cathy Medich, executive director of Commercenet, a Government and industry organization based in Menlo Park, Calif., that hopes to establish standards for commercial transactions on the Internet and other networks.

The idea is to make such data communications immune to wiretaps, electronic eavesdropping and theft by scrambling the transmissions with a secret code — a security technique known as data encryption.

While Commercenet and other organizations have been working to develop a standard for the automated data encryption of commercial transactions, the small band of recent college graduates who formed the Net Market Company in New Hampshire appear to be the first to implement such technology successfully.

Tests of Commercenet's encryption system, which is based on algorithms — mathematical formulas — developed by RSA Data Security Inc. of Redwood City, Calif., are expected to begin this fall.

Commercenet hopes to create an easy-to-use industry standard for protecting Internet transactions.

For now, Net Market's approach is available to the limited number of computer users who have work stations running the Unix software operating system and a sophisticated Internet navigational program called X-Mosaic. The data encryption program is called PGP, for Pretty Good Privacy, which is based on the same RSA algorithms used by Commercenet.

PGP is available free, but it requires technical expertise to download it from the Internet. But within a few months commercial versions of PGP are expected to be available for personal computers using the Windows and Macintosh operating systems, which comprise the vast majority of computers in North America.

SECURITY BREACHES REPORTED

The widespread adoption of standard data encryption tools cannot come too quickly for many Internet entrepreneurs, who hope to foster new levels of commerce on the rapidly growing network.

Alarmed by increasing reports of security breaches on the Internet, many people and businesses are reluctant to transmit sensitive information, including credit cards numbers, sales information or private electronic mail messages, on the network.

But the use of standard data encryption software, which scrambles messages so they can be read only by someone with the proper software "key," has been hindered by a combination of Government regulations and software patent disputes.

Experts say the PGP encryption software used by Net Market is at least as robust as the so-called Clipper encryption technology that the Clinton Administration has been pushing as a national standard. But unlike the Clipper system, the software keys for opening and reading PGP-encrypted documents is not controlled by the Government.

A version of PGP for individuals is available free through the Massachusetts Institute of Technology, but users must retrieve it from an M.I.T. computer through the Internet.

Organizations wanting to use PGP for commercial purposes must obtain it on the Internet from a company in Phoenix called Viacrypt, a maker of computer security software and hardware tools. Prices for PGP begin at $100 a copy.

A BROWSING FEATURE

One achievement of the young programmers at Net Market was to incorporate PGP into X-Mosaic, the software that many Internet users rely on for browsing through the global network.

X-Mosaic is a software tool that allows the users of Unix computers to browse a service of the Internet called the World Wide Web, where companies can post the electronic equivalent of a glossy color brochure with supporting sales or marketing documents.

In the case of Noteworthy Music, the record retailer that leases a "store front" in Net Market's Internet computer, a shopper can look at color pictures of CD album covers.

Mr. Kohn, a 1994 honors graduate in economics from Swarthmore College, came up with the idea for Net Market during his junior year abroad, at the London School of Economics. There, he persuaded an American classmate, Roger Lee, to join his venture.

Mr. Lee, who graduated from Yale this past spring with a degree in political science, is president of the company. For technical expertise, they recruited two other partners from Swarthmore, Guy H. T. Haskin and Eiji Hirai.

The four men live upstairs in the house in Nashua, commuting downstairs each morning to run the business. Because of the pressures of running the system and debugging the software, they rarely venture outside, even though they have a backyard swimming pool.

"We don't get much sun," Mr. Kohn said, "but we're down to a case of Coke a day."

'AN IMPORTANT STEP'

Although Net Market has been selling various products like CD's, flowers and books for several months on behalf of various merchants, yesterday was the first time they had offered digitally secure transactions.

"I think it's an important step in pioneering this work, but later on we'll probably see more exciting things in the way of digital cash," said Philip R. Zimmermann, a computer security consultant in Boulder, Colo., who created the PGP program.

Digital cash, Mr. Zimmermann explained, is "a combination of cryptographic protocols that behave the way real dollars behave but are untraceable."

In other words, they are packets of worth that have value in cyberspace, the same way dollars have value in the real world, except that they have the properties of anonymity, privacy and untraceability. Many details remain to be worked out, Mr. Zimmermann said.

For now, Mr. Brandenberger, despite his historic transaction yesterday, will be paying with plain old dollars, when he gets his credit card bill. And sometime today, the Sting CD will arrive by fairly conventional means — shipped FedEx from the Noteworthy Music warehouse in Nashua.

Alger Hiss, Divisive Icon of the Cold War, Dies at 92

OBITUARY | BY JANNY SCOTT | NOV. 16, 1996

ALGER HISS, THE ERUDITE DIPLOMAT and Harvard-trained government lawyer who was convicted of perjury in an espionage case that became one of the great riddles of the Cold War, died yesterday at Lenox Hill Hospital in New York City. He was 92 and lived in Manhattan.

In a case that catapulted Richard M. Nixon to national attention and helped lay the groundwork for McCarthyism, Mr. Hiss was accused in 1948 of having been a Communist spy while working in the State Department in the 1930's.

By the time the charge surfaced in the late 1940's, Mr. Hiss had accompanied President Franklin D. Roosevelt to the Yalta Conference, played an important role in the founding of the United Nations and left the Government to become president of the Carnegie Endowment for International Peace.

He denied the accusations in a sensational series of Congressional hearings and two trials that mesmerized the public, pitting the slender, self-possessed patrician against his portly, rumpled accuser, Whittaker Chambers, a Time magazine editor and onetime Soviet agent.

The evidence was strange and dramatic: microfilm in a hollowed-out pumpkin, the telltale tracks of an old Woodstock typewriter, a birdwatcher's excited recollection of a rare sighting of a prothonotary warbler.

Mr. Hiss was convicted of perjury in 1950 and served 44 months in prison. He spent the rest of his life trying to clear his name, his reputation seeming to wax and wane with each new turn in the fortunes of Mr. Nixon. The case, meanwhile, became a source of obsessive fascination, a tangle of conspiracy theories and lingering doubts that inspired the kind of interest later seen among Kennedy assassination buffs and followers of the O. J. Simpson murder case.

It was a kind of morality play that severed society along ideological and emotional lines. At Mr. Hiss's death, nearly 50 years after he was first publicly accused, followers of the case remained bitterly split over whether he was guilty, innocent or something in between.

To many, Mr. Hiss was a traitor whose case proved beyond doubt the existence of Communist penetration of the Government. As the columnist George Will put it, Mr. Hiss's claim to innocence had become "one of the long-running lies of modern American history."

Others had come to suspect that Mr. Hiss had lied, but were inclined to excuse him on the grounds that the times had changed, that steps taken to help the Soviet Union during the rise of Hitler in the 1930's might have been condoned at that time, but looked quite different in the late 1940's after the Soviet takeover of Eastern Europe, the start of the Cold War and widespread disclosure of Stalin's crimes.

To still others, many of them on the left, Mr. Hiss was what William Reuben, a friend and the author of one of the dozens of books on the case, called "an American saint": an idealistic New Dealer and rising star in the foreign policy establishment whose career was ruined when he was framed, in part to discredit the New Deal.

In recent years, scraps of purported evidence have continued to surface: declassified government documents, accounts of the contents of Soviet archives. Each time, one side or the other has claimed either to have sealed the case for innocence or to have unearthed a long-sought smoking gun.

Tony Hiss, Mr. Hiss's son, until recently a staff writer for The New Yorker, described his family's experience as "like living inside a fairy tale, with a curse that couldn't be lifted." As Mr. Chambers himself once put it, the case became "a permanent war."

"The Hiss case reveals in stark terms the national mood at the time it occurred," said John Morton Blum, a professor of history emeritus at Yale. "It became significant because of the times and it remains significant for what it says about the times."

Born in Baltimore on Nov. 11, 1904, Alger Hiss was the product of a certain uneasy gentility, the fourth of five children of an executive in a wholesale dry-goods company who committed suicide when Alger was 2 years old, leaving his children to be raised by their mother and an unmarried aunt.

He graduated from the Baltimore public schools and Johns Hopkins University and spent his summers on the Eastern Shore of Maryland. At Harvard Law School, he became a protege of Prof. Felix Frankfurter, who arranged for him to work as a clerk for Associate Justice Oliver Wendell Holmes of the Supreme Court upon graduating in 1929.

In 1933, at Mr. Frankfurter's urging, Mr. Hiss joined President Roosevelt's New Deal Administration, working first in the Agricultural Adjustment Administration, then as counsel to a Congressional committee investigating the munitions industry, then in the Justice Department.

He moved to the State Department in 1936, became director of the Office of Special Political Affairs and served as an American adviser at the Yalta Conference in 1945, in which Roosevelt, Churchill and Stalin drew the map of postwar Europe, setting the stage for the Cold War.

Mr. Hiss was also an organizer of the conferences that laid the foundation and drafted the charter for the United Nations, and was chief adviser to the United States delegation at the first meeting of the General Assembly in 1946. Later that year, he left government to become president of the Carnegie Endowment for International Peace.

THE CHAMBERS CHARGES: DISLOYALTY AND SUBVERSION

The accusations against Mr. Hiss first surfaced publicly on Aug. 3, 1948, when Whittaker Chambers appeared voluntarily before the House Un-American Activities Committee and testified that he had worked during the 1930's as a courier for an elite underground Communist organization in Washington.

Mr. Chambers, who had become a fervent anti-Communist after leaving the Communist Party in 1938, testified that the underground organization's aim had been to install Communists and their sympathizers in government posts. One member, he said, was Mr. Hiss.

Alger Hiss testifying in 1948.

Under oath, Mr. Hiss denied having been a Communist or knowing anyone named Whittaker Chambers. So the committee brought the men together at the Commodore Hotel in New York City. There, Mr. Hiss identified Mr. Chambers as George Crosley, a freelance writer he said he had known in the mid-1930's. Crosley was one of several aliases that Mr. Chambers had used during his Communist years.

The committee then staged a dramatic confrontation between the two men in a marble-columned caucus room in Washington packed with more than 500 people. Under hours of questioning and the glare of klieg lights, the two men differed widely in their accounts of their earlier contacts.

Mr. Hiss said Mr. Crosley had first approached him as a freelance writer looking for information for articles. He said he had sublet an apartment to Mr. Crosley, lent him money and given him the use of an old Ford, but that the relationship had ended badly when Mr. Crosley turned out to be a deadbeat.

Mr. Chambers, however, said Mr. Hiss had given the car to the Communist Party for organizational work. He described Mr. Hiss as his closest friend in the party. He testified that when he decided to quit, he went to Mr. Hiss's house and tried unsuccessfully to persuade him to leave too.

He knew details of Mr. Hiss's life that seemed to suggest close association. For example, he had told the committee in private how Mr. Hiss and his wife, Priscilla, were birdwatchers and had once excitedly recounted how they had spotted a rare prothonotary warbler.

A member of the committee who played an increasingly prominent role in the hearings was Mr. Nixon, a first-term Republican Congressman from California, who said years later that, without the Hiss case, he would never have become Vice President, and then a Presidential candidate in 1960.

At the Washington hearing, Mr. Hiss challenged Mr. Chambers to make his charges outside of the hearing room, without Congressional immunity. So when he was asked about his charges on the radio program "Meet the Press," Mr. Chambers answered: "Alger Hiss was a Communist and may be now."

THE SLANDER SUIT: ACCUSATIONS OF ESPIONAGE

Mr. Hiss sued him for slander. In a deposition in the case, Mr. Chambers broadened his allegations.

He accused Mr. Hiss of espionage: stealing State Department documents and passing them to him for transmission to Moscow. He produced handwritten notes in Mr. Hiss's writing and dozens of pages of State Department dispatches from 1937 and 1938 that he said Mrs. Hiss had retyped.

In an episode that came to define the case, Mr. Chambers then led Federal agents to his Maryland farm and to the so-called pumpkin papers: two strips of developed film and three rolls of undeveloped film containing State and Navy Department documents, hidden in a hollowed-out pumpkin.

Mr. Hiss, summoned before a grand jury, denied that he had given documents to Mr. Chambers or had seen him after January 1937. Because the statute of limitations on espionage had expired, the grand jury indicted him on two counts of perjury, accusing him of lying about his dealings with Mr. Chambers.

A first trial, in 1949, ended in a hung jury, split 8 to 4 for conviction. But in a second trial, which began in November 1949, Hede Massing, who had been prevented from testifying the first time, testified that she had been a Soviet agent and had known Mr. Hiss to be a Communist in 1935. On Jan. 21, 1950, he was convicted. Four days later, he was sentenced to five years in prison.

When Secretary of State Dean Acheson said in a news conference that day that he did not intend to turn his back on Alger Hiss, a little-known Republican Senator named Joseph R. McCarthy seized on the comment to begin charging that the State Department was "thoroughly infested" with Communists.

"Alger Hiss's conviction gave McCarthy and his supporters the essential touch of credibility, making their charges of Communist involvement against other officials headline copy instead of back-page filler," Allen Weinstein, a historian, wrote in his 1978 book, "Perjury: The Hiss-Chambers Case."

Mr. Hiss's court appeals failed and he was sent to the Federal penitentiary in Lewisburg, Pa. He became a model prisoner. With characteristic wry stoicism, Mr. Hiss later described his prison years to his son as "a good corrective to three years at Harvard."

He emerged in late 1954, jobless and disbarred, with Congress about to deny him his pension. His marriage foundered. He and his wife separated in 1959. He eventually found work, selling stationery and printing services to businesses.

"He said he wasn't a great salesman, but he could get in any door," Tony Hiss recalled in a recent interview. "Because when the boss heard that Alger Hiss was in the lobby, he wanted to see what he looked like."

But the scrutiny faded as time passed. By the time the New School for Social Research in New York City hired Mr. Hiss in 1967 to do a series of lectures on the New Deal, the school received only one outraged letter and one telephone call. Five hundred people turned out for the first lecture.

In 1972, he enjoyed a rare victory in the courts. A Federal court overturned the so-called Hiss Act, the law that Congress had passed to bar him from collecting a pension.

All along, he had been trying to clear his name. While still in prison, he had filed a motion for a new trial, arguing that the typewriter used as evidence against him had been tampered with, equipped with a new typeface and planted. The court, unconvinced, had denied the motion.

In 1957, Mr. Hiss published a book, "In the Court of Public Opinion," arguing his case once again, and accusing Mr. Nixon and other Republicans of having attacked him to influence elections and discredit the Yalta agreement and the New Deal.

Mr. Hiss cooperated with many of the authors of the numerous books written on the case, including Mr. Weinstein, who, with the American Civil Liberties Union, filed suit under the Freedom of Information Act to get access to F.B.I. and Justice Department records of the Hiss case.

When the Government finally began releasing the papers, Mr. Hiss used them as grounds for one more petition to the court, claiming prosecutorial misconduct. But Judge Richard Owen ruled in July 1982: "The trial was a fair one by any standard, and I am presented with nothing requiring a hearing on any issue. The jury verdict rendered in 1950 was amply supported by the evidence, the most damaging aspects of which were admitted by Mr. Hiss."

Mr. Hiss appealed, unsuccessfully, to the Second Circuit Court of Appeals and the United States Supreme Court. On Oct. 11, 1983, the Supreme Court declined to hear the case, seeming to put an end to Mr. Hiss's last hope of vindication in the courts.

Meanwhile, Mr. Weinstein, who had started out believing Mr. Hiss might have been innocent, ended up concluding in his book that Mr. Hiss had lied. Several earlier books had sided with Mr. Hiss, but

Mr. Weinstein's was taken by many critics to be the most definitive account.

In the book, Mr. Weinstein tried to address each of the theories that had been floated about the case, from a half-dozen possible conspiracies to the suspicion that Mr. Weinstein said was held for a time by some of Mr. Hiss's own lawyers: that Mr. Hiss was covering for his wife.

"We may expect that newer and perhaps more ingenious defenses of Hiss will soon follow, if only because none of the many theories raised during the past three decades has proved persuasive," he wrote. "There has yet to emerge, from any source, a coherent body of evidence that seriously undermines the credibility of the evidence against Mr. Hiss."

The 1980's brought a resuscitation of the reputation of Mr. Chambers, whom Mr. Hiss's lawyers had tried to discredit during the second trial by calling as a witness a psychiatrist who had concluded from Mr. Chambers' writings and testimony that he suffered from a condition described as "psychopathic personality."

Mr. Chambers himself had gone on to write eloquently of his unhappy life in his 1952 best seller, "Witness," which began with a foreword in the form of a letter to his children, part of which read, "My children, as long as you live, the shadow of the Hiss Case will brush you. In every pair of eyes that rests on you, you will see pass, like a cloud passing behind a woods in winter, the memory of your father — dissembled in friendly eyes, lurking in unfriendly eyes. Sometimes you will wonder which is harder to bear: friendly forgiveness or forthright hate. In time, therefore, when the sum of your experience of life gives you authority, you will ask yourselves the question: What was my father?"

Mr. Chambers died of a heart attack in 1961 at age 60. President Reagan awarded him a posthumous Medal of Freedom in 1984. In 1988, the Reagan Administration declared the farm that had yielded the pumpkin papers a national historic landmark.

THE NIXON CONNECTION: SEARCH FOR SMOKING GUN

When President Nixon's image, too, improved in those years, he appeared at the annual Halloween dinner of a group called the Pumpkin Papers Irregulars, made up mostly of neoconservative followers of the case, and delivered a talk that he later published, entitled "Lessons of the Alger Hiss Case."

When Mr. Nixon died in April 1994, Mr. Hiss released a statement that was striking in its brevity and apparent restraint: "He left many deeds uncorrected and unatoned for," Mr. Hiss said, adding that he felt sympathy for Mr. Nixon's family.

Attention turned to the case once more in the early 1990's after the fall of Communism. Gen. Dmitri Volkogonov, a Russian historian in charge of K.G.B. and military-intelligence archives, announced in 1992 that he had searched files and had found no evidence that Mr. Hiss had been a Communist spy.

"You can tell Mr. Alger Hiss that the heavy weight can be lifted from his heart," General Volkogonov said, responding to a request for information from Mr. Hiss and his supporters, who say a half-dozen other Russian archivists have told them they, too, found no evidence that Mr. Hiss was a spy.

But when American historians questioned whether General Volkogonov's certainty was realistic, given the voluminousness and complexity of the Soviet archives, he conceded that he could not rule out the possibility that some records had been overlooked or even destroyed.

In 1993, Maria Schmidt, a Hungarian historian doing research on the Hungarian secret police, said she had discovered a stack of documents among the restricted files of the Interior Ministry in Budapest that seemed to implicate Mr. Hiss as a Communist spy.

The documents included statements by Noel H. Field, who had worked with Mr. Hiss at the State Department in the 1930's while spying for the Soviet Union. Mr. Field, who later fled to Hungary and was imprisoned, had told the secret police that Mr. Hiss had tried to recruit him as a spy.

Mr. Hiss's detractors pronounced the Hungarian papers the smoking gun that finally validated their view and closed the case.

But his supporters cited evidence that Mr. Field's statements had been coerced.

Then earlier this year, the National Security Agency released a collection of newly declassified documents, including an intercepted message sent by a Soviet spy in Washington to Moscow in 1945, identifying a high-level State Department official present at Yalta as an agent, code-named Ales.

The cable said the agent had worked for Soviet military intelligence since 1935 and had flown on to Moscow after the Yalta conference. There was a notation on the document, by someone at the National Security Agency, suggesting that Ales was "probably Alger Hiss."

Once again, Mr. Hiss's detractors said the document was new proof that he had been a spy. Mr. Hiss released a statement denying he was Ales. Yes, he had spent a night in Moscow after Yalta, but he said he had gone there mainly to see the subway system.

By the time he died, Mr. Hiss had outlived most of the people in the case. His first wife had died in 1984. In addition to their son, Tony, of Manhattan, Mr. Hiss is survived by his second wife, Isabel Johnson of Manhattan; a stepson, Dr. Timothy Hobson of San Francisco, and a grandson.

In addition to several dozen books, the case inspired a documentary film, a television mini-series and at least one play. A novel based on the case was published earlier this year. A new biography of Whittaker Chambers and a new edition of Mr. Weinstein's book are due out in 1997.

Looking back, those who believe that Mr. Hiss was not guilty insisted he would never have accepted their support all those years had he not been telling the truth. In his long insistence, they found final proof. They said he had lived his life like an innocent man.

As for those who believe him guilty, some said they had long ago given up their hope that he would come clean. As William F. Buckley Jr., the founder of National Review, who viewed Whittaker Chambers as a moral hero and never doubted Hiss's guilt, put it recently: "It's probably understandable that he would feel that he had let too many people down."

Code Set Up to Shield Privacy of Cellular Calls Is Breached

BY JOHN MARKOFF | MARCH 20, 1997

A TEAM OF WELL-KNOWN computer security experts will announce on Thursday that they have cracked a key part of the electronic code meant to protect the privacy of calls made with the new, digital generation of cellular telephones.

The announcement, intended as a public warning, means that — despite their greater potential for privacy protection — the new cellular telephones, which transmit streams of digital information in code similar to computer data, may in practice be little more secure from eavesdropping than the analog cellular phones, which send voice as electronic patterns mimicking sound waves, that have been in use the last 15 years.

It was such eavesdropping, for example, that caused trouble for Newt Gingrich when a Florida couple listened to his cellular phone conversation in December about the Congressional ethics inquiry.

Now that digital wireless networks are coming into use around the nation, the breaking of the digital code by the team of two computer security consultants and a university researcher confirms fears about privacy that were raised five years ago when the communications industry agreed under Government pressure to adopt a watered-down privacy technology.

Several telecommunications industry officials said the pressure came from the National Security Agency, which feared that stronger encryption technology might allow criminals or terrorists to conspire with impunity by cellular phones.

But independent security experts now say that the code is easy enough to crack that anyone with sufficient technical skills could make and sell a monitoring device that would be as easy to use as a police scanner is.

Such a device would enable a listener to scan hundreds of wireless channels to listen in randomly on any digital call within a radius ranging from 1,000 feet to a number of miles. Or, as with current cellular technology, if a specific person was the target of an eavesdropper, the device could be programmed to listen for any nearby digital call to that person's telephone number.

Other possible transgressions would include using the device to automatically harvest all calling card or credit-card data transmitted with nearby digital wireless phones.

And, because of a loophole in the Communications Act of 1934, making and selling such devices would not be illegal, though actually using one would technically be against the law.

These monitoring devices are not yet available, but security experts said that a thriving gray market was certain to develop. And with technical details of the security system already circulating on the Internet, instructions for cracking it will almost certainly make their way into the computer underground, where code breaking and eavesdropping are pursued for fun and profit.

Technical details of the security system were supposed to be a closely guarded secret, known only to a tight circle of industry engineers. But the researchers performed their work based on technical documents that were leaked from within the communications industry and disseminated over the Internet late last year.

"The industry design process is at fault," said David Wagner, a University of California at Berkeley researcher who was a member of the team that broke the code. "We can use this as a lesson, and save ourselves from more serious vulnerabilities in the future."

Communications industry technical experts, made aware of the security flaw earlier this year, have been meeting to determine whether it is too late to improve the system's privacy protections. Already the digital technology is in use in metropolitan areas, including New York and Washington, where either the local cellular networks have been modified to support digital technology or where new so-called wireless personal communications services are being offered.

"We're already in the process of correcting this flaw," said Chris Carroll, an engineer at GTE Laboratories, who is chairman of the industry committee that oversees privacy standards for cellular phones.

But Greg Rose, a software designer for the Qualcomm Inc., a leader in digital cellular systems, said that fixing the flaw would be "a nightmare." Tightening the security system, Mr. Rose said, would involve modifying software already used in the computerized network switching equipment that routes wireless digital telephone calls, as well as the software within individual phones.

Currently, about 45 million Americans have cellular phones, though most of them so far are based on an older analog standard that offers no communications privacy. But cellular companies are gradually converting their networks to the new digital standard, and the new personal communications services networks going into operation around the country also employ the digital-encryption system. Nearly a million P.C.S. phones have been sold in the United States, according to cellular industry figures.

Besides Mr. Wagner, the other researchers who cracked the code were Bruce Schneier and John Kelsey of Counterpane Systems, a Minneapolis consulting firm. Mr. Schneier is the author of a standard textbook on cryptography.

The new digital wireless security system, which was designed by cellular telephone industry engineers, was never intended to stop the most determined wiretappers.

But because digital calls are transmitted in a format corresponding to the one's and zero's of computer language, they are more difficult to eavesdrop on than conventional analog calls, which are transmitted in electronic patterns. And digital calls protected with encryption technology — basically a mathematical formula in the software that scrambles the signal — would be all the harder for a third party to listen to surreptitiously.

Because the encryption system that the industry adopted in 1992 was deliberately made less secure than many experts had recommended at the time, privacy rights advocates have been warning since that the code could be broken too easily. An announcement Thursday that the code has indeed been cracked would seem to bear out those concerns.

"This should serve as a wake-up call," said James X. Dempsey, senior staff counsel for the Center for Democracy and Technology, a public interest group. "This shows that Government's effort to control encryption technology is now hindering the voice communications industry as well as the data and electronic communication realm."

Industry executives acknowledged that steps must be taken to address the problem.

"We need strict laws that say it is illegal to manufacture or to modify a device which is designed to perpetrate the illegal interception of P.C.S. telephone calls," said Thomas E. Wheeler, president of the Cellular Telephone Industry Association, a Washington-based trade group.

Mr. Wheeler said the weaker privacy technology had been adopted not just to appease the Government but because makers of wireless communications hardware and software wanted to embrace a technical standard that would meet export regulations. Those rules, based on national security considerations, sharply curtail the potency of American-made encryption technology.

The three computer researchers who broke the code belong to an informal group of technologists who believe strongly that powerful data-scrambling technologies are essential to protect individual privacy in the information age. These technologists, who planned to release their findings in a news release on Thursday, argue that the best way to insure that the strongest security codes are developed is to conduct the work in a public forum. And so they are sharply critical of the current industry standard setting process, which has made a trade secret of the underlying mathematical formulas used to create the security codes.

"Our work shows clearly why you don't do this behind closed doors," Mr. Schneier said. "I'm angry at the cell phone industry because when they changed to the new technology, they had a chance to protect privacy and they failed."

Mr. Carroll, head of the industry's privacy committee, said it planned to revise the process for reviewing proposed technical standards.

Tommy Flowers, 92, Dies; Broke Nazi Codes

OBITUARY | BY RICHARD GOLDSTEIN | NOV. 8, 1998

TOMMY FLOWERS, A BRITISH civil servant with a genius for electronics whose pioneering Colossus computers enabled the Allies to decode top-level German military communications in World War II, died on Oct. 28 at his home in London. He was 92.

The Colossus machines were once described by Mr. Flowers as a "string-and-sealing-wax affair." But they became the capstone of the intelligence operation known as Ultra, which outwitted the Germans and, in the words of Gen. Dwight D. Eisenhower, "saved thousands of British and American lives."

Soon after Britain went to war with Germany in the summer of 1939, many of its leading mathematicians, cryptographers and technicians were assembled at Bletchley Park, a Victorian-era estate 55 miles north of London. It was there that the German military codes were broken.

Mr. Flowers was named a Member of the British Empire, receiving a $1,000 award for the decoding of military messages from the German Enigma machines in the war's early years.

But his major contribution came in 1944 and 1945, when the computers he designed tackled the codes produced by the more sophisticated German Lorenz machines. The deciphering of those messages, between Hitler's headquarters and his generals, gave the British and Americans insight into German defenses for the D-Day invasion and subsequent battles.

Thomas Harold Flowers was born on Dec. 22, 1905, in London, where his father installed bakery machines. Early on, he showed a penchant for engineering. As his son Kenneth related, "When he was age 5 he was told he'd just gotten a baby sister. He said, 'I'd rather have a No. 5 Meccano,' " a construction kit.

Mr. Flowers obtained a degree in engineering from the University of London and in the late 1930's experimented with electronic telephone transmissions for the research arm of the British Post Office, which oversaw the nation's communications.

He was enlisted in the Bletchley Park effort in 1942, although he later developed his computer at the Post Office's Dollis Hill research station in London.

The British deduced the principals behind the Lorenz codes, but had been frustrated in developing technology for quick decoding. The machine the British were using in 1943 was slow and unreliable, and sometimes caught fire.

Over a period of nine months, working with several senior engineering aides and a few dozen technicians, Mr. Flowers developed the first large electronic-valve computer, overcoming the skepticism of Bletchley Park officials.

Colossus measured 16 feet by 7 feet, weighed one ton and was put together partly with standard telephone-exchange parts, the "string and sealing wax." Although primitive by today's standards, it quickly pinpointed the wheel settings used by the Germans' Lorenz machine operators for coded messages, an essential first step in deciphering. Another device then completed the decoding.

"As soon as they delivered the machine to Bletchley Park in December 1943, it was a sensation," said Prof. Brian Randell of the University of Newcastle-upon-Tyne, an authority on the program. "It was an incredibly revolutionary idea."

Decades later, Mr. Flowers wrote how "at the time I had no thought or knowledge of computers in the modern sense and had never heard the term used except to describe somebody who did calculations on a desk machine."

Churchill's Government wanted 10 Colossus devices delivered by early June 1944, for the D-Day invasion. At least 10 machines were in operation by the war's end, but only one more Colossus could be produced in time for the Allied invasion of Normandy, on June 6. That machine was, however, five times as fast as the first Colossus, which started work the previous December.

After the war, British authorities dismantled most of the Colossus machines. The very existence of Bletchley Park and the Colossus computers remained secret until the 1970's.

Mr. Flowers returned to his electronics research for the Post Office and remained there until 1964. He then worked for a division of International Telephone and Telegraph, before retiring in 1969.

In addition to his son Kenneth, of Beverley, England, he is survived by his wife, Eileen; another son, John, of London, and three grandchildren.

Professor Randell remembered how Mr. Flowers was "very quiet and modest" when finally allowed by British authorities to reveal his accomplishments.

"He had to come to terms with the fact that he was now being encouraged to talk about something that he'd been very actively discouraged from almost thinking about for 30 years," Professor Randell observed.

Although recognized by the scientific community, Mr. Flowers remained largely unknown to the British public. Yet his work lives on at Bletchley Park, which is now a tourist attraction. Run by a historic trust, it displays the Germans' Enigma and Lorenz machines. But the centerpiece is a replica of the Colossus computer, which was switched on by the Duke of Kent — in the presence of Mr. Flowers — on June 6, 1996, the 52d anniversary of the D-Day invasion, which marked the beginning of the end for Nazi Germany.

Code Talkers' Story
Pops Up Everywhere

BY TODD S. PURDUM | OCT. 11, 1999

GALLUP, N.M., OCT. 9 — They are old men now, drifting into town in their boots, blue jeans and silver belt buckles. Like other aging veterans of World War II, they meet once a month on Saturday mornings for a blend of poignant and prosaic duties: planning parades, disbursing money for the funeral expenses of one old comrade and a small scholarship for the son of another and reviewing the coffee budget, $21.69 this month.

But more than 50 years ago, the 15 men in the Chamber of Commerce hall by the railroad tracks here were young United States marines who fought fiercely for the flag of a country that had given their people nothing but grief. And the embroidery on the battered red and yellow caps covering their grizzled heads and tanned faces proclaims their proud name: Navajo Code Talkers.

In some of the toughest battles of the South Pacific, 400 of these men — most of them barely out of high school on the reservation just north of here, part of it in New Mexico and part in — transmitted thousands of radio messages in a code based on their intricate and unwritten language, in which fighter planes became "hummingbirds," dive bombers "chicken hawks" and submarines "iron fish." Though the Japanese repeatedly broke other American military codes, they never came close to cracking the Navajos', which remains one of the handful of codes in military history that were never deciphered.

In fact, the Navajos' secret was considered so valuable that it was kept classified until 1968, and their singular contribution to the wartime efforts of what has been called "the greatest generation" went largely unheralded. Fewer than half the code talkers are still alive. But suddenly, it seems, their story is popping up everywhere.

It was the subject of a recent documentary on television's History Channel. It is celebrated in "The Code Book" (Doubleday, 1999), Simon

Singh's history of cryptography. The Smithsonian Institution has asked for help in putting together a display about the code talkers in its new museum of Indian history on the Mall in Washington.

Not one but two Hollywood films are in the works. One is being developed in cooperation with the code talkers by a group of Native American filmmakers and Gale Anne Hurd, the producer of the "Terminator" movies and "Armageddon." The other is being developed by John Woo, the action-adventure director from Hong Kong.

"Now that they've seen these documents, everyone wants to interview code talkers," said Samuel Billison, president of the Navajo Code Talkers Association and a member of his tribe's governing council. "There's a lot of interest, and not just in the United States. I just got a call from Italy the other day."

The code talkers' achievements are the stuff of high drama. Their work was the brainchild of Philip Johnston, a World War I veteran and engineer who had grown up as the son of missionaries on the Navajo reservation and learned the language as a child. In 1942, he persuaded Marine officers in San Diego to test the idea, and after a period of bureaucratic indecision 29 initial recruits were inducted and began training.

From the beginning, the idea was not simply to transmit messages in Navajo, a singsong and subtly inflected descendant of northern Asian languages that is easily susceptible to mispronunciation, but to create a unique code based on Navajo words. Military terminology created a special challenge; hence the avian equivalents for aircraft. To enable other words ("Guadalcanal," for example) to be spelled out, each letter of the English alphabet was assigned a Navajo equivalent ("a" was "ant," or "wol-la-chee"). To keep the Japanese from deciphering the code by analyzing the frequency of common letters like "e," alternative words representing the same letter were added to the mix.

The system worked beautifully. In the first 48 hours of the battle of Iwo Jima alone, Navajos sent and decoded 800 messages without an error. The presence of the Indian marines, some of whom looked and sounded decidedly Asian, in the Pacific Theater caused some complications; more than once, code talkers were briefly mistaken for Japanese soldiers by their American comrades.

Sometimes the similarities had almost comic consequences, as when Paul H. Blatchford, a code talker from Fort Defiance, Ariz., was mistaken for Japanese by an enemy soldier who heard him on the radio in Iwo Jima.

"He said, 'Where are you from?' " recalled Mr. Blatchford, an electrical engineer who at 82 is the oldest surviving code talker. "He said, 'Talk English,' and he thought we were Japanese. One of my buddies heard me and he said, 'What the hell are you talking about?' I lied and told the Japanese guy that the Japanese artillery was not hitting our guns, and said, 'Tell your guy to move about 15 degrees to the east.' "

The war was a transforming experience for men like Mr. Blatchford and Mr. Billison, who came home and went to school on the G.I. Bill of Rights, ultimately earning a doctorate in school administration from the University of Arizona and spending 30 years as a teacher and administrator in public and Indian schools. But postwar life was not easy for everyone. Today the code talkers got the news that one of the original 29 recruits, Alfred Leonard, had recently died in Seattle without enough money to have his body shipped back to the reservation for burial.

So the association wrote a check for $467 (which reduced its general fund balance to an even $2,000), collected $90 in cash in a baseball cap passed around the table and gave it all to Mr. Leonard's nephew. Later, a $500 grant to help the son of a member attend vocational school in Albuquerque depleted their shoestring balance still further.

Another code talker, John Brown, expressed soft-spoken alarm at recent statements by New Mexico's Governor, Gary E. Johnson, a Republican, questioning the effectiveness of law-enforcement efforts against drugs and floating the notion of decriminalizing or even legalizing drugs so they could be regulated like alcohol.

"I think it would be an appropriate time to defend our Navajo youths and other youths against some of this publicity," Mr. Brown said before the group passed a unanimous resolution deploring the Governor's comments. "He's got some bad advice for the youngsters."

Since the association was formed in 1971, code talkers have marched in parades from Presidential inaugurals to the Tournament of Roses, though these days, more ride than walk. President Ronald Reagan designated Aug. 14 Navajo Code Talkers Day in 1982, and members of the group regularly appear before school and veterans' groups to tell their story. But their wartime experiences also remain painful and private for many of the veterans, and when today's meeting ended, most scattered quietly, declining to stop and talk with a visiting reporter.

Mr. Billison said some members were wary of having their story exploited without compensation, and he pointed to one of the Hollywood proposals as a prime example. Mr. Woo, the action director, is reportedly trying to persuade Nicolas Cage, who was in Mr. Woo's hit movie "Face/Off," to star in "Windtalkers," the story of a code talker and his Marine bodyguard. During the war, the Navajos had bodyguards charged with protecting them from capture by the Japanese, with standing orders to kill them if necessary to protect the code, though none ever had to. Mr. Cage would play a bodyguard assigned to a code talker.

But Mr. Billison thinks that is a backward way to tell the story, and he has drafted a letter asking Mr. Cage not to take the part.

"I told him to reconsider," he said, "for the dignity of the Navajo."

CHAPTER 5

2000–Present: Challenges of the 21st Century

Today, security breaches on the internet have become a concern for the government and the commercial sector. Scholars and educators are exploring the history of cryptography through art and museum exhibits. Writers examine the contributions of women such as the famed abolitionist and spy Harriet Tubman and the lesser-known female cryptographers of World War II. China uses its technological power to exert control over its population, and security officials say Russian intelligence services are using a blend of propaganda, hacking attacks and disinformation to try and destabilize Europe. Intelligence efforts on behalf of China, Russia and Saudi Arabia have raised alarm bells for domestic and foreign governments alike.

Cryptologists Discover Flaw in E-Mail Security Program

BY JAMES GLANZ | MARCH 21, 2001

TWO CRYPTOLOGISTS ANNOUNCED yesterday that they had found a flaw in the most widely used program for sending encrypted, or coded, e-mail messages. If confirmed, the flaw would allow a determined adversary to obtain secret codes used by senders of encrypted e-mail.

The program, called P.G.P. for Pretty Good Privacy, is used by human rights organizations to protect vulnerable sources, by corporations to ensure secure communications and by millions of individual users. American security experts cautioned that they could not fully judge the accuracy of the claim, which was issued in Prague, before more technical details become available. The experts also noted that some sort of access to the sender's computer — either directly or via the Internet — would be needed to exploit any such flaw.

According to a statement issued yesterday by ICZ, an information technology company in Prague with about 500 employees, the cryptologists, Vlastimil Klima and Tomas Rosa, found the problem while doing research on secure communications for the Czech government.

"It is very serious," said Kriz Zdenek, general manager of ICZ.

Mark McArdle, vice president of P.G.P. engineering at Network Associates in Santa Clara, Calif., which licenses the encryption program to corporate and individual users, said he had already assigned a team of engineers to check out the claim, which he learned of yesterday from a journalist.

"We are very eager to both analyze this and respond to it," Mr. McArdle said. "We want to make sure that our systems are completely robust."

He expressed surprise that the Czech company did not inform him of the problem so that a software fix, often called a patch, could be made available with the announcement of any bug. But Miroslav Votruba, marketing director at ICZ, said several e-mail messages informing Network Associates of the problem more than a week ago received no response.

"We are willing to cooperate before the algorithm or description of the problem will be released on the Web," Mr. Votruba said.

P.G.P. relies on a type of cryptography that uses two separate keys, one to encode a message and one to decode it. The flaw claimed by the cryptographers does not involve cracking the code itself, which is considered virtually invulnerable, but would work around it by allowing an intruder to steal one of the keys held privately by a user.

Without such a flaw or bug, the private key would be unavailable even to an intruder who gained access to a computer, because it exists there only in scrambled form. The ICZ announcement says there is a way to unscramble it but gives few details. Mr. McArdle said such a bug would mainly affect the coded electronic "signatures" that allow the recipient to verify the sender's identity. In effect, it would allow the intruder to impersonate the sender in future communications.

"This is probably real," said Bruce Schneier, founder and chief technology officer of Counterpane Internet Security in San Jose, Calif., referring to the bug. But he said it showed that e-mail security involved more than simply protecting the message in transit on the Internet.

Dr. Michael A. Caloyannides, a senior fellow at Mitretek Systems in McLean, Va., said the bug would be "a bit of a shock," since P.G.P. had been considered essentially invulnerable. And Matthew Zimmerman, project coordinator for the Science and Human Rights Program of the American Association for the Advancement of Science, confirmed that his organization routinely used P.G.P. to protect dissidents and informers around the world.

But even if the problem does turn out to be serious, said Jonathan Zuck, president of the Association for Competitive Technology in Washington, an industry group involving information technology, security-conscious Internet users should not panic.

"This kind of technology arms race is always a factor in any new technology standard," Mr. Zuck said, adding that the eventual result should be an improved encryption program.

Veiled Messages of Terror May Lurk in Cyberspace

BY GINA KOLATA | OCT. 30, 2001

THE INVESTIGATION OF the terrorist attacks on the United States is drawing new attention to a stealthy method of sending messages through the Internet. The method, called steganography, can hide messages in digital photographs or in music files but leave no outward trace that the files were altered.

Intelligence officials have not revealed many details about whether, or how often, terrorists are using steganography. But a former French defense ministry official said that it was used by recently apprehended terrorists who were planning to blow up the United States embassy in Paris.

The terrorists were instructed that all their communications were to be made through pictures posted on the Internet, the defense official said.

The leader of that terrorist plot, Jamal Beghal, told French intelligence officials that he trained in Afghanistan and that before leaving that country for France, he met with an associate of Osama bin Laden. The plan was for a suicide bomber to drive a minivan full of explosives through the embassy gates.

The idea of steganography is to take advantage of the fact that digital files, like photographs or music files, can be slightly altered and still look the same to the human eye or sound the same to the human ear.

The only way to spot such an alteration is with computer programs that can notice statistical deviations from the expected patterns of data in the image or music. Those who are starting to look for such deviations say that their programs are as yet imperfect but that, nonetheless, some are finding widespread use of steganography on the Internet. For national security reasons some of these experts do not want to reveal exactly what they find, and where.

"Quite an alarming number of images appear to have steganography in them," said one expert who has looked for them, Chet Hosmer, the president and chief executive of WetStone Technologies in Cortland, N.Y.

Mr. Hosmer says his company has not decided whether to reveal all the sites where he is finding steganography. He has found it on the auction site eBay, where people can post pictures anonymously, inserting hidden messages if they choose to, and just as anonymously download them, retrieving the messages. WetStone works under a contract to the Air Force.

At George Mason University, Dr. Neil F. Johnson, a steganography expert, said he became so worried by steganography's potential to be used by terrorists and criminals that he stopped publishing his research on how to detect it, reasoning that if people knew how he detected it, and where, they could devise methods to thwart him and move their messages to sites he has not checked.

"I have no reason to think that Al Qaeda is not using steganography," Dr. Johnson said, but he, like others, pointed to no proof. His research, he said, is financed by "law enforcement."

"I think it's foolish to disclose what I'm scanning for, whether I'm scanning and whether I'm detecting anything," Dr. Johnson said. "To give that away tips one's hands."

Steganography, Greek for "hidden writing," is one of the most ancient ways of passing secret messages, but until very recently few computer scientists paid it much attention — it seemed more a relic of ancient times, sort of a Paul Revere-type "one if by land two if by sea" way of sending information.

The ancient Greeks used it, writing a message on a wooden tablet and covering the wood with wax. Sentries would think the tablets were blank, but when they were delivered, their recipients would simply scrape off the wax and read the message.

In World War II, Dr. Johnson said, the Allies became so suspicious about hidden messages that the United States Office of Censorship "took extreme actions, such as banning flower deliveries which contained delivery dates, crossword puzzles and even report cards."

But in recent years, steganography has arrived on the Internet in a big way, experts said, with free and easy-to-use programs to insert messages into music or picture files. Many programs also allow users to choose an encryption scheme to further hide the message, so even if the recipients know it is there, they have to decode it to read it.

"In the past two years, the number of steganography tools available over the Internet has doubled — it's 140 and growing," Dr. Johnson said. Some of the newer ones, he said, prompt users at each step on how to proceed.

Bruce Schneier, a founder of Counterpane, an Internet security company, likened steganography to what is known as a dead drop — a message, money or papers left in a hiding place to be picked up by someone.

"The effect is that the sender can transmit a message without ever communicating directly with the receiver," Mr. Schneier wrote in a recent newsletter. "There is no e-mail between them, no remote log-ins, no instant messages. All that exists is a picture posted in a public forum, and then downloaded by anyone sufficiently enticed by the subject (both third parties and the intended receiver of the secret message.)"

Mr. Hosmer said he became interested in steganography three years ago when he conducted a study for the Air Force looking at potential areas for cybercrime and cyberterrorism.

"We wanted to see what kinds of tools and weapons were being used by terrorist organizations," he said. To his surprise, he said, steganography, an area he had paid little attention to, stood out because it could be so effective in hiding the very fact that people were communicating — thwarting attempts to detect terrorist activities by looking for flurries of communications between members.

Mr. Hosmer found more than 100 free steganography programs on the Internet and said he was shocked when the providers of the programs said there had been over a million downloads of the technology.

"It really struck us: why were there so many downloads?" Mr. Hosmer said. Some, he said, may be hackers or people who are using it for fun. But, he said, he doubts that those are the only users.

"We said, 'This is really startling, that there are so many people who are communicating without people knowing that they are communicating.' And because these programs were coming from around the world, we were very concerned."

Mr. Hosmer's company began looking at millions of digital pictures that were posted on the Internet. They scanned auction sites and pornographic sites, where people can post and download digital images anonymously.

"We started getting hits," Mr. Hosmer said, adding that about 0.6 percent of millions of pictures on auction and pornography sites had hidden messages. The messages they found on eBay were encrypted and unreadable, he said. The company also noticed that some of the same photos seemed to be used over and over again, with different messages each time. "If you're very sophisticated at this, you would never use an image again," Mr. Hosmer said.

One limitation in published steganography detection programs is that often they miss images hidden in the most frequently used format, JPEG, said Dr. Jessica Fridrich, a research professor at the Center for Intelligent Systems at the State University of New York at Binghamton.

It is hard to see evidence of steganography in such files because the detection methods look for statistical evidence that an image's data have been distorted. But JPEG files are distorted by their very nature — the digital data are altered when the files are compressed to send them electronically.

Dr. Fridrich said that a steganography detection program she developed also had that limitation but that she had greatly improved the program so that, even though it still did not work well for JPEG images, it was much better at finding images in other formats. She said she was providing it to the Air Force, which was paying for her group's work. "I believe that the Air Force made this program available to other government agencies," she said.

The best published method for finding steganography in JPEG files, Dr. Fridrich said, is one developed by Niels Provos, a graduate student at the University of Michigan. Mr. Provos said he had seen no steganography in the two million images from eBay he had examined.

On the other hand, Mr. Provos can miss steganography — he said he had trouble finding small messages and was unable to detect a short message in a photograph that was sent to him. He was told beforehand that an unencrypted message had been inserted.

Mr. Provos publishes his research, enabling others to know how he detects steganography and, as a consequence, how to avoid his detection system. "When I started my research, which was a couple of years ago, it was, of course, in a completely different political situation," he said.

Now, he says, he asked himself again if publication was advisable. He concluded it was, arguing that research thrived when people could freely exchange ideas.

Of course, those whose business it is to intercept terrorist communications would never reveal anything they have learned about steganography.

Asked what the National Security Agency — the nation's codemaking and codebreaking agency — knows, Dr. Robert Morris, a retired cryptographer who was chief scientist there, said, "We wouldn't talk about it."

Codebook Shows an Encryption Form Dates Back to Telegraphs

BY JOHN MARKOFF | JULY 25, 2011

IF NOT FOR A computer scientist's hobby of collecting old telegraph code-books, a crucial chapter in modern cryptography might have been lost to history.

The collector is Steven M. Bellovin, a professor of computer science at the Columbia University School of Engineering and a former computer security researcher at AT&T Bell Laboratories. On a recent trip to Washington he found himself with a free afternoon and decided to spend it at the Library of Congress, looking for codebooks that weren't in his collection.

In the 19th century codebooks were used not so much for secrecy as for compression, to bring down the prohibitive cost of telegraph communication. (The first trans-Atlantic cables cost $5 a word.) Designers devised lists of words to replace phrases and even sentences.

But when Dr. Bellovin hunted though the card catalog, his interest was piqued by an 1882 codebook whose title included the word "secrecy."

"I thought, 'O.K., let me go see how they did it,' " he recalled. "When I read the two-page preface, my jaw dropped."

He could plainly see that the document described a technique called the one-time pad fully 35 years before its supposed invention during World War I by Gilbert Vernam, an AT&T engineer, and Joseph Mauborgne, later chief of the Army Signal Corps.

Although not widely used today because it is relatively difficult to work with, the one-time pad is still viewed as one of strongest ways to encrypt a communication. The technique is distinguished by the use of a random key, shared by both parties, to encode the message and decode it; the key must be used only once and then securely disposed of.

It was the Soviet Union's misuse of the technique — code clerks were occasionally reusing the one-time pads instead of discarding them — that led to the Venona project, the collaboration between the United States and British intelligence services that yielded code-cracking coups during World War II and the cold war.

The 1882 monograph that Dr. Bellovin stumbled across in the Library of Congress was "Telegraphic Code to Insure Privacy and Secrecy in the Transmission of Telegrams," by Frank Miller, a successful banker in Sacramento who later became a trustee of Stanford University. In Miller's preface, the key points jumped off the page:

"A banker in the West should prepare a list of irregular numbers to be called 'shift numbers,' " he wrote. "The difference between such numbers must not be regular. When a shift-number has been applied, or used, it must be erased from the list and not be used again."

That sent the astonished Dr. Bellovin to the Internet to try to find out whether Mr. Miller's innovation was known to the later inventors.

The results of his largely online detective work can be found in the July issue of the journal Cryptologia. Born in Milwaukee in 1842, Mr. Miller attended Yale and then joined the Union Army, where he fought at Antietam and was wounded at the Second Battle of Bull Run.

He was transferred to the Army inspector general's office, where he became a member of a squad of detectives investigating Lincoln's assassination — perhaps his first contact with cryptanalysis, Dr. Bellovin speculates. He seems to have kept a diary that still belongs to his descendants, but Dr. Bellovin was unable to obtain it.

According to several independent specialists in cryptography, Mr. Miller was undoubtedly the first to propose the concept of the one-time pad.

"Miller probably invented the one-time pad, but without knowing why it was perfectly secure or even that it was," said David Kahn, the author of the definitive 1967 book "The Codebreakers." "Moreover, unlike Mauborgne's conscious invention, or the Germans' conscious adoption of the one-time pad to superencipher their Foreign Office

codes, it had no echo, no use in cryptology. It sank without a trace —
until Steve found it by accident."

Dr. Bellovin found no evidence that either Mr. Vernam or Mr.
Mauborgne ever met Mr. Miller, but he did uncover one more tanta-
lizing clue — in the society pages of The San Francisco Chronicle, of
all places. At a military ball at the Presidio in 1907, Mr. Miller met
Parker Hitt, a cryptographer who was a student and colleague of Mr.
Mauborgne's.

"It is quite certain that if Hitt knew of Miller's system," Dr. Bellovin
writes, "he would have shared that knowledge with Mauborgne when
they were together at the Army Signal School in Fort Leavenworth."
But as he acknowledges, that is still a big "if."

Scientists Expand Scale of Digital Snooping Alert

BY JOHN MARKOFF | SEPT. 4, 2013

SCIENTISTS REPORTED ON WEDNESDAY that they had taken a step toward bringing improved security to computer networks, developing an encryption technique that will extend protection to a small group of computer users.

The researchers at Toshiba's European research laboratory in Cambridge, England, in a paper published on Wednesday in the journal Nature, wrote that they had figured out a way to allow a group of users to exchange encryption keys — long numbers that are used to mathematically encode digital messages — through an experimental technique known as quantum key distribution.

The new technique is believed to be more practical and less expensive than existing technologies. It also extends the scale of the current quantum key systems to as many as 64 computer users from just two users.

The system does not prevent eavesdropping — it simply serves as a kind of burglar alarm, alerting computer users that an outsider is listening to a transmission on an optical network.

Nevertheless, the advance comes at a time of growing concern about the relative ease of breaching computer security, prompted by recent disclosures based on the documents leaked from the National Security Agency and the British Government Communications Headquarters intelligence agencies by Edward J. Snowden. One worry is that the initial exchange of the key material in modern encryption systems has become vulnerable.

Today many digital encryption systems are based on the ability of two computer users to secretly exchange a "key" — a large number, which is then used to establish a secure communication channel to exchange messages over a computer network.

The encryption key is encoded in a special stream of photons or bits. The Toshiba work is based on the ability to make the infinitesimally short time measurements required to capture pulses of quantum light hidden in streams of photons transmitted over fiber optic links — and to do that in a network of dozens of users.

The key exchange is usually protected by the use of mathematical formulas based on the challenge of factoring large numbers. In recent years public key cryptographic systems have been improved by lengthening the factored numbers used in the formula. That, in principle, would require vastly more computing resources to break into the system.

Quantum cryptography relies instead on encoding the key in a stream of quantum information — photons that are specially polarized. If a third party eavesdrops on the communication, the fact will be immediately obvious to the parties of the secret communication.

"One of the attractive things about quantum cryptography is that security comes in the form of the laws of nature," said Andrew J. Shields, one of the authors and the assistant managing director for Toshiba Research Europe. "It should, in principle, be secure forever."

Encryption systems that are now commercially available are used to secure the wires over which digital information is transferred, but they are costly and function only over limited distances. Allowing multiple users to share a network connection while using a quantum encryption system could significantly lower costs, Dr. Shields said.

He acknowledged that a quantum encryption system solved only a portion of the problem.

"To be honest, quantum cryptography allows us only to know if someone is tapping the fiber," he said. "There are other areas of concern."

But the eavesdropping that the system is designed to detect has been well documented. For example, in 2006 an AT&T technician came forward to report that the National Security Agency had established such a system to monitor communications traffic flowing through an

AT&T network switching facility in San Francisco. Had a quantum cryptography system been in place, Dr. Shields said, the N.S.A. presence would have been detected.

Dr. Shields said that he could not speak publicly about whether Toshiba would try to commercialize the research work of his group. The group, he said, now plans to extend the range of the system further and use it in a live computer network.

Alan Turing, Enigma Code-Breaker and Computer Pioneer, Wins Royal Pardon

BY EMMA G. FITZSIMMONS | DEC. 24, 2013

NEARLY 60 YEARS after his death, Alan Turing, the British mathematician regarded as one of the central figures in the development of the computer, received a formal pardon from Queen Elizabeth II on Monday for his conviction in 1952 on charges of homosexuality, at the time a criminal offense in Britain.

The pardon was announced by the British justice secretary, Chris Grayling, who had made the request to the queen. Mr. Grayling said in a statement that Mr. Turing, whose most remarkable achievement was helping to develop the machines and algorithms that unscrambled the supposedly impenetrable Enigma code used by the Germans in World War II, "deserves to be remembered and recognized for his fantastic contribution to the war effort and his legacy to science."

The British prime minister, David Cameron, said in a statement: "His action saved countless lives. He also left a remarkable national legacy through his substantial scientific achievements, often being referred to as the 'father of modern computing.' "

Mr. Turing committed suicide in 1954, two years after his conviction on charges of gross indecency. He was 41. In a 1936 research paper, Mr. Turing anticipated a computing machine that could perform different tasks by altering its software, rather than its hardware.

He also proposed the now famous Turing test, used to determine artificial intelligence. In the test, a person asks questions of both a computer and another human — neither of which they can see — to try to determine which is the computer and which is the fellow human. If the computer can fool the person, according to the Turing test, it is deemed intelligent.

In 2009, Prime Minister Gordon Brown issued a formal apology to Mr. Turing, calling his treatment "horrifying" and "utterly unfair." But Mr. Cameron's government denied him a pardon last year.

An online petition urging a pardon received more than 35,000 signatures. The campaign has also received worldwide support from scientists, including Stephen Hawking.

When Mr. Turing was convicted in 1952, he was sentenced — as an alternative to prison — to chemical castration by a series of injections of female hormones. He also lost his security clearance because of the conviction. He committed suicide by eating an apple believed to have been laced with cyanide.

The queen has the power to issue a "royal prerogative of mercy" to pardon civilians, but rarely does so. Mr. Grayling said that Mr. Turing's sentence would today be considered "unjust and discriminatory."

Mr. Turing has been the subject of numerous biographies, as well as "Breaking the Code," a play based on his life that was presented in London's West End and on Broadway in the 1980s.

Security Secrets, Dated but Real

MUSEUM REVIEW | BY EDWARD ROTHSTEIN | AUG. 1, 2014

ANNAPOLIS JUNCTION, MD. — Was the National Cryptologic Museum designed using a code of some kind? Something perhaps meant, cryptically, to mask its character and significance? Something that can be deciphered only by those familiar with mysterious organizations like the Black Chamber?

This is, after all, a museum created and run by the National Security Agency, a peculiar governmental body: Its existence was once scarcely acknowledged; its 1952 founding documents were once completely classified; and its finances were once buried deep in a "black budget." But with Edward J. Snowden's release of stolen classified files, along with reportorial histories by James Bamford, the N.S.A. is now partly revealed; it is popularly portrayed as an agency unhampered by oversight, secretly probing every aspect of our data-saturated lives.

Yet here, just down the road from that agency's black-box buildings with their thousands of workers and immense parking lots, we come upon this quaint, slightly old-fashioned, flat-topped structure that looks like a converted motel, which it is.

And when you enter, instead of facing evidence of untrammeled technological power, you are greeted with a rack of informative booklets and children's activity sheets, almost as if invoking tourist brochures from the building's previous incarnation.

The quaintness continues: The first exhibit, about "hobo communication," is a model-train-size diorama of a small New England town.

Is "hobo" perhaps the code word for a data-mining project that tracks smartphones? Does it refer to a cipher machine like Enigma? No, it means what it says: When hobos used the rails to travel the country, they would scrawl warning signs to fellow travelers on walls and walkways. A jagged line meant "barking dog here"; a circle with an X inside meant "good place for a handout." Hobo code. We press buttons and see lights go on where the signs appear.

Maybe there really is a bit of agency coding involved, too. Just as when it opened in 1993, this museum is the agency's only public face, so the hobo exhibit may be meant, in part, to disguise or humanize the caricature. It also sets the tone for the museum, which is stylistically dated, slightly ramshackle and cramped. But it is also thoroughly engrossing, offering a compelling survey of American cryptography.

It is redacted, of course, and its content deliberately dated. You never get close to anything redolent of classified technologies or Snowden-esque controversies. And you never quite shake the feeling that maybe if you touched a wall sconce, the cabinets would pull back, revealing a cyberwarfare lab.

But such fantasies quickly fade, because the material here spurs the imagination in so many other directions. These artifacts are as various and seemingly miscellaneous as the markings on an encoded document. Here, in 13,000 square feet, is a 16th-century copy of the first published book on cryptology, Johannes Trithemius's "Polygraphiae," along with a cipher disc used by the Confederacy during the Civil War; children's school notebooks used by the Vietcong to cloak intelligence on fighting forces; and a heliograph, whose maneuverable mirrors were used in the First World War to flash sunbeams in Morse Code patterns.

There is a portion of the United States Navy Bombe, built by the National Cash Register Company in Dayton, Ohio, in 1943: an early mechanical computer, whose tangle of wires and whirring gears were used to break the German code. There are also, remarkably, two working German Enigma machines, whose intricacies led a generation of Polish, British and American code breakers into intricate explorations, with thousands of lives at stake. You can type on them now and watch the keys light up in a code once thought unbreakable.

The museum's curator, Patrick D. Weadon, noted in a conversation that the museum's unspecified budget was modest. You feel that, too. Acquisitions, donations and expanding ambitions have led to recently

The National Cryptologic Museum has a gallery devoted to early spy satellites.

added displays about the Civil and Revolutionary Wars. But over all, the tight space jumbles the dense narrative so you have to unspool it as you maneuver.

Yet it works. The museum's old-fashioned wall-panel style is suited to its theme. Here we see cryptology as a craft, dependent as much on insight as on technology. "They served in silence" reads one memorial to fallen agency employees, but in a series of displays, some silence falls away — at least for the retired or deceased. We see portraits of brilliant linguists who could learn languages in a weekend, along with images of female and African-American analysts whose genius also allowed them to break constraining social codes.

The historical examples of cryptologic invention are remarkable: During the Revolutionary War, a letter sent by the British general Sir Henry Clinton seemed to be supporting a particular military maneuver, unless you placed an hour-glass-shaped cutout, whose use was prearranged, over the page: The message showing through means

A Frostburg computer, circa 1991.

just the opposite. Activities for children invite similar exercises, but this is no game. The pivotal 1942 Battle of Midway might have been lost if the United States hadn't begun to break Japan's code; the war in the Pacific could well have ended in American surrender.

There is recurring emphasis here, too, on language. We begin to understand coding as an unusual form of translation: It turns sense (the message) into non-sense (the code). The job of decryption is much harder: to discern pattern in the midst of noise, meaning in seeming chaos.

As we approach the present, those tasks become more and more daunting, keeping pace with the technology. We see sections of a supercomputer that was installed at the N.S.A. in 1993: the Ziegler, from Cray Research. It was, we read, "among the most powerful super-computers in the world." The piece on display weighs 7,495 pounds. It required a 60-ton refrigeration unit. And how powerful was it? Its processor speed is now dwarfed by a smartphone's. It had just 32 gigabytes of memory, and its disk storage was 142 gigabytes. I'll stick with my laptop.

What happens to cryptology during 20 years of such transformation? In a gallery devoted to the evolution of intelligence satellites and secure communications, we see the changes in hardware, but it is the processing that becomes extraordinary. And that we can't see (or are not cleared to).

Still, we know enough to imagine what is happening. Contemporary cryptology leaves General Clinton's cutout and the Enigma's turning discs far behind. A particular message may not even be the point any longer. The larger challenge is to identify that transmission amid noisy background chatter. And more important than any single message may be the patterns and anomalies discerned as vast quantities of data are churned. A secret in this world might be best preserved by seeming not to be a secret at all.

That's the comfort I take in recent revelations about the N.S.A.'s engorgement on communications data. It may not care much about the isolated case — the individual, say, worried about privacy. The problem is that the quantities of data are so great that anomalies are almost certain. Something may seem to have coded significance when it does not. And that would sweep even the innocent into a cryptographic world determined to discern meaning, even if, on occasion, there is none.

The National Cryptologic Museum is at 8290 Colony Seven Road, Annapolis Junction, Md.; 310-688-5849, nsa.gov.

Cracking Codes through the Centuries

BY WILLIAM GRIMES | FEB. 3, 2015

WASHINGTON — The Sigaba encryption machine squats in the Folger Shakespeare Library here like a thuggish interloper. Used by the American military in the 1940s and 1950s to send coded messages, it looks like an oversize, boxy typewriter with rotors rising above the lid like a mechanical brain. No object could seem less Elizabethan, yet appearances deceive.

"Decoding the Renaissance: 500 Years of Codes and Ciphers," an exhibition that runs through Feb. 26, draws a straight line from the cipher discs devised by the humanist polymath Leon Battista Alberti in the 1460s and Francis Bacon's discovery of bilateral ciphers — a way of writing coded messages with just two letters — to Sigaba, the American answer to the German Enigma machine.

"Decoding the Renaissance," at the Folger Shakespeare Library in Washington, includes two early books on cryptography.

It's a rather fashionable subject at the moment. "The Imitation Game," and Benedict Cumberbatch's performance as Alan Turing, the British mathematician who broke the Enigma code, has transmitted the allure of cryptography to millions of moviegoers. The subject's mystique has drawn unusual visitors to "Decoding the Renaissance," like the F.B.I.'s cryptanalysts, not the typical audience for a library devoted to Shakespeare and his contemporaries.

Together, the Folger Library and the Library of Congress, a major lender to the exhibition, hold one of the world's deepest collections of works on cryptography. This material constitutes the spine of the show, which sets forth the basic principles of code-making, a topic of fevered study during the Renaissance.

"It was a period of cold war, in effect," said Bill Sherman, the head of research at the Victoria & Albert Museum in London and a professor of Renaissance studies at the University of York, who organized the exhibition. The Pan-European tensions between Protestant and Roman Catholic states, the rise of international trading systems and the newfound importance of diplomatic missions demanded spy networks, secrecy and subterfuge — "all the things you get in a John le Carré novel," Mr. Sherman said.

The exhibition includes the earliest printed book on cryptography, "Polygraphiae Libri Sex," written by the Benedictine abbot Johannes Trithemius and published in 1518, as well as a coded letter from Francis Walsingham, Elizabeth I's spymaster. A letter from George Digby, the Second Earl of Bristol, on behalf of Charles I, reports on the progress of rebel forces under Oliver Cromwell using a set of substitutions known as a nomenclator. The number 154, for example, means "danger," and p5 means "with."

One of the rarest books in the exhibition is "A New Method of Cryptography" (1666), written during the English Civil War by Samuel Morland. His proposal for a cyclologic cryptographic machine, illustrated on the book's last page, relies on a series of cipher wheels that make it a close cousin to Sigaba and Enigma.

A Sigaba encryption machine used by the American military during World War II is also part of the Folger exhibition.

Not all codes depended on letters and numbers. Steganography — literally "hidden writing" — provided an alternate set of tools for practitioners of the espionage trade. John Wilkins's "Mercury, or the Secret and Swift Messenger," published in 1641, suggests writing with the "juice of glow-worms" to create messages that can be read only in the dark, or "glutinous moisture" — milk or fat — that the recipient can read by scattering dust on the letters. Alphabets could be translated into musical notes or flowers.

The road to modern cryptography leads through the stupendous brain of William F. Friedman, chief cryptologist for the American military in both world wars and a primary focus of the exhibition.

Mr. Friedman, whose family emigrated from Kishinev, Russia, as the threat of pogroms mounted, started out as a plant geneticist. That career path was derailed when, in 1915, he joined Riverbank

Laboratories, a research institute founded by the eccentric textile magnate George Fabyan.

Mr. Fabyan subscribed to the popular theory that Francis Bacon had written the works attributed to Shakespeare and had embedded coded clues to that effect in the First Folio and other texts. Mr. Fabyan assigned a team to work on the project. Mr. Friedman met and married one of the Bacon researchers, Elizebeth Smith, and quickly became drawn into the world of cryptography, for which he displayed an almost supernatural talent.

The Friedmans gave up on the Bacon theory, which they debunked in 1957 in the book "The Shakespearean Ciphers Examined," but Riverbank's Bacon research made it an ideal cryptographic training center for military personnel during the First World War. The exhibition includes a panoramic photograph of the school's Class of 1918, whose members line up to spell out Bacon's maxim "Knowledge is power" in a code expressed by the way their heads are turned. There were only enough students, however, to spell "Knowledge is pow."

After serving in France as the cryptographer for Gen. John J. Pershing, Mr. Friedman became the chief cryptanalyst for the Army. As the leader of the Signals Intelligence Service, in the 1930s and 1940s, he helped decipher the Japanese cipher machine Purple — he built a replica by analyzing its encrypted messages — and, with his associate Frank Rowlett, developed Sigaba. The machine, which contained 15 encrypting rotors to Enigma's five, was undecodable and remained classified until 2000.

Mr. Friedman took a playful approach to cryptography. The exhibition includes one of his annual encrypted Christmas cards; a coded menu from the "Café Cryptanalytique," presented to dinner guests at his home; and a secret message hidden in sheet music for "My Old Kentucky Home."

He kept one foot in the Renaissance until the end of his life, a connection that explains the centerpiece of the exhibition, the mysterious Voynich manuscript. The document, an illustrated codex written in an unknown language and script in northern Italy in the early 15th century, is named after Wilfrid Voynich, the Polish antiquarian bookseller who acquired it in 1912.

It has never been decoded, though Mr. Friedman spent four decades trying. The illustrations suggest that it might be a scientific treatise, with sections on medicinal herbs, astronomy and other subjects, but no one can be sure. "You could think of it as the ultimate work of outsider art," said Michael Witmore, the Folger's director.

The manuscript was donated to the Beinecke Rare Book & Manuscript Library at Yale in the 1960s. Mr. Friedman did not find the key to the Voynich code but he did have a theory. It was, he thought, an early effort to create an artificial language. He communicated this idea in a Friedman-esque way, concealing it in a 1959 article on Chaucer's anagrams, then putting the solution in an envelope to be opened after his death.

"Decoding the Renaissance: 500 Years of Codes and Ciphers" continues through Feb. 26 at the Folger Shakespeare Library, 201 East Capitol Street SE, Washington; 202-544-4600, folger.edu.

What the Country Owes Harriet Tubman

OPINION | BY BRENT STAPLES | JULY 17, 2015

AMERICAN CAPITALISM IS DEEPLY implicated in slavery. The traffic in human beings produced profits, not just for plantation families, but for bankers, merchants, manufacturers and insurance companies that issued policies on slaving vessels and the lives of the people who were carried in their holds.

Treasury Secretary Jacob Lew may not have had this connection in mind when he announced last month that the $10 bill was about to be refurbished and would soon feature the likeness of "a woman who has contributed to and represents the values of American democracy."

But the relationship between capitalism and slavery has come into sharper focus since the abolitionist and Union Army spy Harriet Tubman became the runaway favorite to replace Andrew Jackson on the twenty-dollar bill.

Jackson's fortunes fell last month, when the former Federal Reserve Chairman Ben Bernanke recommended that the federal government preserve Hamilton on the ten — because he helped create the Constitution and was a visionary in terms of economic policy — and dump Jackson from the twenty because he was a "man of many unattractive qualities and a poor president" who also opposed attempts to establish a central bank. Given Jackson's aversion to central banking, Mr. Bernanke said, he "would probably be fine with having his image dropped from a Federal Reserve note."

Mr. Bernanke did not enumerate Jackson's "unattractive qualities." But among them were his staunch support of slavery, his antipathy for Native Americans — many of whom died horrible deaths after being evicted from their ancestral lands in the South — and an unfortunate tendency toward self-dealing in financial matters.

Harriet Tubman.

Tubman, by contrast, was a champion of freedom. Not long after escaping slavery in Maryland she started returning to the South, organizing escapes for scores of enslaved people who often fled to freedom just ahead of armed posses.

And, as the New Yorker writer Amy Davidson wrote earlier this week:

> When the Civil War broke out, Tubman put her knowledge of the back routes of the South into the service of the United States Army, as a scout and a spy. Among other things, the intelligence she provided proved crucial in the capture of Jacksonville, Florida — a town named for a certain President who is now on the twenty, and who, in 1835, among other pro-slavery acts, gave Southern postmasters the authority to seize Abolitionist literature that passed through the mail. For what was hopefully not the last time, Tubman beat Jackson.

Ms. Davidson reminds us that Tubman's valor was widely recognized during her lifetime. Secretary of State William H. Seward wrote: "I have known her long as a noble high spirit, as true as seldom dwells in the human form." In 1899, when Tubman was in her 70s, Congress passed a bill raising her pension in recognition of her military service. The text of the bill featured testimonials from three battlefield generals.

Harriet Tubman is more than worthy of a place on the national currency. In granting it, the country would be acknowledging the role that slavery played in the building of the republic and celebrating a woman who lived out democracy's highest ideals at a time when it was worth one's life to do so.

BRENT STAPLES has been a member of the Times editorial board since 1990.

Cryptography Pioneers Win Turing Award

BY JOHN MARKOFF | MARCH 1, 2016

SAN FRANCISCO — In 1970, a Stanford artificial intelligence researcher named John McCarthy returned from a conference in Bordeaux, France, where he had presented a paper on the possibility of a "Home Information Terminal."

He predicted the terminal would be connected via the telephone network to a shared computer, which in turn would store files that would contain all books, magazines, newspapers, catalogs, airline schedules, public information and personal files.

Whitfield Diffie, then a young programmer at the Stanford Artificial Intelligence Laboratory, read Mr. McCarthy's paper and began to think about the question of what would take the place of an individual signature in a paperless world. Mr. Diffie would spend the next several years pursuing that challenge and in 1976, with Martin E. Hellman, an electrical engineer at Stanford, invented "public-key cryptography," a technique that would two decades later make possible the commercial World Wide Web.

On Tuesday, the Association for Computing Machinery announced that the two men have won this year's Turing Award. The award is frequently described as the Nobel Prize for the computing world and since 2014, it has included a $1 million cash award, after Google quadrupled its size.

This year, it was announced during the RSA Conference, a security technology symposium held here this week.

Named for Alan Turing, the British mathematician and computer scientist, the award is particularly noteworthy because it comes at a time that the Federal Bureau of Investigation is locked in a bitter feud with Apple over the agency's inability to unlock the cryptographic system that protects digital information stored in the company's iPhones.

While private information can be protected with a so-called "symmetric" key, or a single digital code, that is used to mathematically scramble the data, the problem becomes much more difficult when two parties who have not met physically wish to have a secret interaction.

The privacy protection technology that is now used extensively to protect modern electronic communications is based on Mr. Diffie's and Mr. Hellman's original research that led to the creation of "public-key cryptography" technology.

Public-key cryptography is a method for scrambling data in which each party has a pair of keys, one which can be publicly shared and the other which is known only to the intended recipient of a message. It is possible for anyone to encrypt a message using the individual's public key. However, the message can only be unscrambled with the aid of the private key held securely by the recipient of the message.

In the United States and elsewhere, cryptography was once a highly classified military and intelligence agency technology. But in the 1970s academic researchers began delving into the field, which led to clashes with law enforcement and spy agencies.

In 2013, documents released by Edward J. Snowden, the former government contractor, revealed widespread government surveillance of Internet traffic, leading companies like Apple and Google to modify the security in their products and to the current fight between Apple and the F.B.I.

Mr. Diffie and Mr. Hellman have long been political activists. Mr. Hellman has focused on the threat that nuclear weapons pose to humanity, and he said in an interview he would use his share of the prize money to pursue work related to the nuclear threat. He said he also planned to write a new book with his wife on peace and sustainability.

Mr. Diffie, who has spent his career working on computer security at telecommunications firms and at the Silicon Valley pioneer Sun Microsystems, has been an outspoken advocate for the protection of personal privacy in the digital age.

He said in an interview that he plans to do more to document the history of the field he helped to create. "This will free me to spend more of my time on cryptographic history, which is urgent because the people are quickly dying off," Mr. Diffie said.

The Women Who Helped America Crack Axis Codes

REVIEW | BY MERYL GORDON | NOV. 6, 2017

Code Girls
The Untold Story of the American Women Code Breakers of World War II
By Liza Mundy
Illustrated. 416 pp. Hachette Books. $28.

IN THE FALL OF 1941, mysterious letters appeared in the mailboxes of a select group of young women attending the Seven Sister colleges. Chosen for their aptitude in such subjects as math, English, history, foreign languages and astronomy, the women were invited to meet one-on-one with senior professors. At Wellesley, the students were asked unusual questions: Did they like doing crossword puzzles, and did they have imminent wedding plans?

Those women who gave the right answers — yes, and no — were asked to sign confidentiality agreements and join a hush-hush government project. With war raging in Europe, the United States Navy had been staffing up its cryptanalysis division for several years but this was a new recruiting strategy. The female undergrads were offered campus training in code breaking, with the promise of government civilian jobs in Washington upon graduation.

In the months after the bombing of Pearl Harbor and America's entry into World War II, such a patriotic summons became more urgent. Not only did the Navy reach out to women from a wider range of colleges but the Army began ramping up its own rival code-breaking unit. After Army brass were chastised for competing with the Navy for the same female campus talent pool, the Army switched tactics and sought out small-town schoolteachers eager to participate in the war effort and take part in a big-city adventure.

In Liza Mundy's prodigiously researched and engrossing new book, "Code Girls: The Untold Story of the American Women Code

Ann Caracristi, far right, oversaw an Army code breaking unit when she was 23.

Breakers of World War II," she describes the experiences of several thousand American women who spent the war years in Washington, untangling the clandestine messages sent by the Japanese and German militaries and diplomatic corps. At a time when even well-educated women were not encouraged to have careers — much less compete with men to demonstrate their mastery of arcane, technical skills — this hiring frenzy represented a dramatic shift. The same social experiment was simultaneously unfolding on the other side of the Atlantic. The British debutantes and their middle-class peers recruited to work at the secret Bletchley Park code-breaking operation came to outnumber the men.

In an era when history is being updated to reflect the math and science accomplishments of 20th-century women with such accounts as Margot Lee Shetterly's "Hidden Figures: The American Dream and the Untold Story of the Black Women Mathematicians Who Helped Win the Space Race," Mundy's book offers valuable insights and information about those unsung women who made crucial contributions during wartime.

Their work was often mind-numbingly tedious and frustrating as the women spent 12-hour days and seven-day weeks in steamy offices staring at incomprehensible columns of numbers and letters and trying to decipher patterns. They learned to recognize ciphers — where one letter is substituted for another letter or number — and to interpret "additives," extra numbers thrown in to stump prying eyes. They built and operated "bombe" machines to decode the thousands of German messages sent out via the complex Enigma machine, work that was done in conjunction with Bletchley Park.

Mundy's narrative turns thrilling as she chronicles the eureka moments when the women succeed in cracking codes, relying on a mixture of mathematical expertise, memorization and occasional leaps of intuition. Thanks to their efforts in retrieving and passing along vital information about enemy battle plans and the whereabouts of Japanese vessels, the American military was able to sink enemy supply ships, shoot down enemy planes and blunt attacks on American targets. This was emotionally fraught work since the women occasionally learned, in advance, that the Japanese had targeted ships in regions where their loved ones were serving. As Mundy writes, "Some of the women broke messages warning about attacks before they happened but were helpless to avert them."

In the run-up to the D-Day landing in Normandy, the women were also charged with creating phony coded American messages to deceive the Germans about the site of the invasion.

A former Washington Post reporter, Mundy was inspired to tackle this book after her husband, Mark Bradley, a veteran Justice Department official, read a declassified World War II document about a counterintelligence operation, which noted that many women schoolteachers worked on the project.

The author of three previous books that touch on feminist themes, Mundy paints a vivid portrait of the daily lives of these energetic single young women — the upheaval and challenges of adjusting to the high-pressure military environment, the condescension and sexism from male colleagues and superiors, the cramped living quarters, the constant anxiety over brothers and boyfriends in harm's way, the wartime romances, weekend high jinks and stress-related breakdowns.

Three-quarters of a century later, with firsthand recollections of World War II vanishing daily in the obituary columns, Mundy was able to track down and interview more than 20 former code breakers such as Ann Caracristi, an English major at Russell Sage College who turned out to be such a problem-solving prodigy that as a 23-year-old she became the head of an Army research unit. Dorothy Braden Bruce, a 97-year-old former Virginia schoolteacher known as Dot, described the tense experience of decoding urgent data from Japanese supply ships and also offered up amusing and poignant details about wartime life.

These accounts are supplemented by numerous oral histories, declassified documents and exhaustive research at the National Archives. Mundy delves deeply into a transitional pre-Betty Friedan moment in American life when institutional discrimination was the norm. As she points out, a 1941 Navy memo proposed paying female clerks, typists and stenographers $1,440 per year, while men in the same posts were to receive $1,620. The gap grew even larger higher up the ladder: Female Ph.D.s were slated for $2,300 salaries compared with $3,200 for their male counterparts.

The author unearths the stories of pioneers like Agnes Meyer Driscoll, a math, physics and language whiz who joined the Navy in 1917, broke Japanese codebooks in the 1920s and '30s and went on to train a generation of male code breakers, only to be patronized and pushed aside during World War II. The talented cryptologist Elizebeth Smith Friedman was hired by the Coast Guard in 1927 to break the code of rumrunners and went on to work for other federal agencies, designing the codes used by the Office of Strategic Services, the predecessor to the C.I.A. Yet her husband, the Army code breaker William Friedman, was sometimes given credit for her work.

In her effort to cram in an enormous amount of information and give so many women their due, Mundy's book suffers at times since it's hard to keep track of her vast cast of characters, many with similar backgrounds. As their stories began to blur, I found myself frequently flipping back to remind myself who was who. When she attempts to tell the tale thematically, her time-shifting can be confusing. At the end of Part Two of the book, it's the summer of 1944, the United States military has just retaken Guam and Dot Braden is feeling optimistic that the Allies are doing well in the Pacific. When Part Three begins a few pages later, we're back in 1943; then the story abruptly zigs to dismal times in 1942.

At the end of the war, virtually all of the female code breakers were given their walking papers and returned to civilian life. Only a few superstars were asked to stay on (among them Caracristi, who went on to become the first female deputy director of the National Security Agency).

For these accomplished and resourceful women, who had been given a heady taste of professional success, it was jarring to have to fight to be accepted to top graduate programs on the G.I. Bill or embark on traditional paths as wives and mothers. Warned not to reveal their secret wartime lives, many remained silent about their valuable service. Thanks to Mundy's book, which deftly conveys both the puzzle-solving complexities and the emotion and drama of this era, their stories will live on.

MERYL GORDON, the director of magazine writing at N.Y.U.'s Arthur L. Carter Journalism Institute, is the author of "Bunny Mellon: The Life of an American Style Legend."

Russia Says He's a Spy. His Lawyer Says He Just Wanted Photos of a Cathedral.

BY NEIL MACFARQUHAR | JAN. 22, 2019

MOSCOW — A former United States Marine who was arrested in Moscow on spying charges had been handed a flash drive that he thought contained pictures of churches but was instead loaded with classified information, his lawyer said on Tuesday.

Paul N. Whelan, 48, was arrested by the Federal Security Service on Dec. 28 in an upscale Moscow hotel where he had been staying for a wedding. After his arrest, it emerged that by birth and through a patchwork of ancestors, he held citizenship from the United States, Canada, Britain and Ireland.

Mr. Whelan, who has denied the charges, was detained in his room minutes after being given a thumb drive containing a full list of names of the employees of a secret Russian security agency, according to reporting early this month by Rosbalt, a news agency close to the security services.

The Russian foreign minister, Sergey V. Lavrov, has described Mr. Whelan as having been "caught red-handed."

Vladimir A. Zherebenkov, Mr. Whelan's lawyer, said that he had been handed the secret information by another person whom he would not identify. He did not say whether Mr. Whelan knew the person, or what motive the person might have had for passing on classified material.

"Paul actually was meant to receive information that was not classified from an individual," Mr. Zherebenkov told reporters before a bail hearing on Tuesday. The drive was supposed to contain pictures, he said.

"These were cultural things — a trip to a cathedral, Paul's holiday," he said. "But as it turned out, it contained classified information."

Mr. Whelan had no clue what was on the drive because he was arrested before he had a chance to look at it, the lawyer said.

Mr. Whelan appeared at Moscow City Court on Tuesday, his first public appearance since his arrest. The session, attended by three consular officials from countries where Mr. Whelan holds citizenship, was closed to the news media.

Mr. Whelan, wearing a sky blue shirt and dark pants, was locked in a glass docket, as is the custom in Russian courts. He did not speak to reporters before they were ushered out of the room. During the hearing he spoke for about 15 minutes in his own defense, the lawyer said.

The judge denied a request for bail and ordered Mr. Whelan held in Moscow's Lefortovo Prison for another month. If convicted of espionage, he faces up to 20 years in jail.

In prison he has an English-speaking cellmate and has been able to check out English-language books from the library by authors like Jack London, Russian prisoner advocates have said.

David Whelan, his twin brother, who lives in Canada, said in a statement that the family would not comment until it had heard more about the hearing from consular officials.

Mr. Whelan has made numerous trips to Russia over a decade, traveling around the country by railroad and cultivating dozens of friends through Vkontakte, a Russia social media platform akin to Facebook. Many of those friends had military backgrounds, and relatives suggested that he might have been seeking out kindred spirits, given his own long service in the Marines.

He had been given a bad conduct discharge in 2008 related to a larceny case.

From the time Mr. Whelan's arrest was made public, there has been speculation in Russia that he was imprisoned in order to exchange him for one or more Russians held in American jails. President Vladimir V. Putin has repeatedly expressed outrage at the United States' detention of Russian citizens.

Mr. Whelan might have been taken, for example, to exchange him for Maria Butina, who pleaded guilty on Dec. 13 in Federal District Court in Washington to a charge of conspiring to act as a foreign agent.

Ms. Butina, 30, admitted to being involved in an organized effort, backed by Russian officials, to try to lobby influential Americans in the National Rifle Association and the Republican Party.

Mr. Whelan's lawyer has said that an exchange was possible and he would welcome it, but that it would take some time, and would require a pardon from Mr. Putin. The shortest possible time for such a case would be six months to a year, he said.

"This is a long process," Mr. Zherebenkov told The New York Times in early January. "I myself hope that we can rescue and bring home one Russian soul."

POLINA OSTRAVSKAYA contributed reporting.

Family of American Imprisoned on Spy Charge in China Appeals for Help

BY CHRIS BUCKLEY AND EDWARD WONG | FEB. 22, 2019

BEIJING — Kai Li, an American businessman born in China, had stepped off a plane in Shanghai, preparing to visit his mother's grave. Instead, Chinese state security officers grabbed him and accused him of spying, and a court later sentenced him to 10 years in prison after a short, secretive trial.

Now, two and a half years after Mr. Li was detained, his family in New York has broken its silence, saying that the espionage conviction against Mr. Li, an exporter of aircraft parts, was groundless and driven by political motives.

In recent years, relations between the United States and China have been tested by trade and technology disputes. The United States has accused China of hacking companies and inducing or bribing scientists to hand over commercial secrets. China has also stepped up warnings against foreign spies and publicized convictions of foreigners on espionage charges.

Harrison Li, Mr. Li's son, said the Chinese authorities had charged his father with providing state secrets to the F.B.I. He says he is sure that his father was not a spy, and that his conviction showed the risks that American visitors to China face as tensions with the United States have festered.

"I certainly hope that the U.S. government will view my father's case as a serious indication of China's willingness to use the coercive and inflammatory tactics of detaining foreign citizens," Harrison Li said by telephone. "It's very clear to us that the nature of the case is political, and tied to whatever geopolitical conflicts exist between the two countries."

At first, Mr. Li's family kept quiet about his case while State Department officials lobbied Chinese officials to release him, the son said. But Mr. Li, 56, went on trial in Shanghai in August 2017 and was convicted and sentenced in July of last year. Harrison Li said that he and his mother decided to speak out after Mr. Li's appeal was rejected last month.

The F.B.I. declined to comment on the case. The Chinese Ministry of Foreign Affairs did not respond on Friday to faxed questions about the case, nor did the police, the prosecutors' office or the foreign affairs office in Shanghai.

The case raises broader questions about how foreign businesspeople dealing with sensitive sectors in China — in this case, the aerospace sector — are vulnerable to espionage charges.

Before Mr. Li's detention, his life centered on his home and businesses on Long Island, where he owned two gas stations. He went to the United States in 1989 after the Tiananmen Square massacre and gained citizenship there in the 1990s, said his son, who graduated from Harvard last year and works in finance. Mr. Li's wife also immigrated from China.

Mr. Li visited China two or three times a year, and he ran a company that exported aircraft parts to China and elsewhere in Asia on behalf of a subsidiary of Boeing, Harrison Li said. The son said he did not know the subsidiary's name, and Boeing had no immediate comment on Friday.

The aerospace sector looms large in the competition between China and the United States, and both governments guard against the theft of secrets. Last year, the United States orchestrated a complex international sting operation to arrest a Chinese intelligence official who was charged with trying to get proprietary information from a GE Aviation employee.

"I'm sure that his business would have made him an easier target for the Chinese government," Harrison Li said of his father. He said his father wrote in a letter, while in detention, that the paperwork for the exports entailed making filings with the United States government that may have drawn suspicion from Chinese investigators.

"The Trump administration must use all tools available to prioritize bringing Mr. Li back home," Senator Chuck Schumer, Democrat of New York, said on Thursday.

Mr. Li's case has added to the tensions between Beijing and Washington.

Relations have been strained since last year, when President Trump hit goods made in China with tariffs intended to force Beijing into dismantling what he and other critics say are unfair trade and investment barriers.

China was also incensed by the arrest in Canada late last year of Meng Wanzhou, the chief financial officer of Huawei, who American prosecutors say helped Huawei slip past American sanctions on Iran by fraudulently misleading a bank. Two Canadian men were detained in China in December in what appeared to be payback for Ms. Meng's arrest.

"The international security competition between the United States and China is beginning to affect the business world in a very significant way," said Evan S. Medeiros, a professor at Georgetown

University who was senior Asia director in the Obama White House.

In targeting American businesses, China has a "much bigger tool kit to play with" because of the vast powers of its state security apparatus and lack of real legal oversight, Mr. Medeiros said, without commenting specifically on Mr. Li's case.

Members of the Trump administration and of Congress have taken up Mr. Li's case, including Secretary of State Mike Pompeo and other State Department officials, Harrison Li said.

"We regularly raise Mr. Li's case with Chinese officials," the State Department said a written statement. It said consular staff had sent multiple requests to the Chinese authorities seeking Mr. Li's release on humanitarian grounds, but received no response.

This week, Senator Chuck Schumer, Democrat of New York, and four members of the House of Representatives sent a letter to Mr. Trump urging him, for a second time, to push the Chinese government to release Mr. Li. The letter, a copy of which was obtained by The New York Times, said, "It is incumbent upon our government to fulfill its responsibility to a citizen in distress and be his vociferous advocate."

Mr. Schumer told The Times on Thursday, "The Trump administration must use all tools available to prioritize bringing Mr. Li back home."

On Friday afternoon, Garrett Marquis, a spokesman for the White House National Security Council, said the United States had appealed to Beijing "multiple times over the past two years for Li Kai's immediate release."

In China, President Xi Jinping has brought in new laws to combat espionage and perceived threats to national security, which include vague and sweeping definitions of national secrets.

In recent years, Chinese security officers have been especially tough in detaining people born in China who have foreign citizenship. Some visitors of Chinese descent have spent years in prison on sweeping charges.

In a travel warning for China reissued last month, the State Department said that American citizens of Chinese heritage could face additional scrutiny and harassment.

When Mr. Li went to trial, United States consular officers were not allowed into the hearing, after the court invoked a rule banning outsiders from sensitive cases involving national security. The hearing lasted a little over an hour, said Harrison Li, who is in touch with the consular officers.

After the trial, the court took the unusual step of ordering additional investigation by the prosecution office, postponing a judgment, Harrison Li said. Such a move suggests that judges thought the evidence presented by the prosecution was insufficient.

Still, the judges last year declared Mr. Li guilty of sharing one "classified" state secret and four "confidential" state secrets, his son said, citing a judgment seen by the United States consulate in Shanghai. Those classes of secrecy both fall below the topmost confidentiality classification in China.

Harrison Li hopes that Mr. Trump will take up his father's case when he next meets with Mr. Xi. But he said he had qualms about speaking out because he was afraid that the authorities might take it out on his father, who has been in poor health with bouts of shingles and constant stomach ailments.

"There's already a very real concern that when families of imprisoned people in China go public, they retaliate," he said. "It just seems that there's not much more that can be done quietly."

CHRIS BUCKLEY reported from Beijing and EDWARD WONG from Washington.

C.I.A. Informant Extracted From Russia Had Sent Secrets to U.S. for Decades

BY JULIAN E. BARNES, ADAM GOLDMAN AND DAVID E. SANGER

PUBLISHED SEPT. 9, 2019 | UPDATED SEPT. 17, 2019

WASHINGTON — Decades ago, the C.I.A. recruited and carefully culti-vated a midlevel Russian official who began rapidly advancing through the governmental ranks. Eventually, American spies struck gold: The longtime source landed an influential position that came with access to the highest level of the Kremlin.

As American officials began to realize that Russia was trying to sabotage the 2016 presidential election, the informant became one of the C.I.A.'s most important — and highly protected — assets. But when intelligence officials revealed the severity of Russia's election interference with unusual detail later that year, the news media picked up on details about the C.I.A.'s Kremlin sources.

C.I.A. officials worried about safety made the arduous decision in late 2016 to offer to extract the source from Russia. The situation grew more tense when the informant at first refused, citing family concerns — prompting consternation at C.I.A. headquarters and sowing doubts among some American counterintelligence officials about the infor-mant's trustworthiness. But the C.I.A. pressed again months later after more media inquiries. This time, the informant agreed.

The move brought to an end the career of one of the C.I.A.'s most important sources. It also effectively blinded American intelligence officials to the view from inside Russia as they sought clues about Kremlin interference in the 2018 midterm elections and next year's presidential contest.

CNN first reported the 2017 extraction on Monday. Other details — including the source's history with the agency and the cascade of doubts set off by the informant's refusal of the initial exfiltration offer — have not been previously reported. This article is based on interviews in recent months with current and former officials who spoke on the condition that their names not be used discussing classified information.

Officials did not disclose the informant's identity or new location, both closely held secrets. The person's life remains in danger, current and former officials said, pointing to Moscow's attempts last year to assassinate Sergei V. Skripal, a former Russian intelligence official who moved to Britain as part of a high-profile spy exchange in 2010.

The Moscow informant was instrumental to the C.I.A.'s most explosive conclusion about Russia's interference campaign: that President Vladimir V. Putin ordered and orchestrated it himself. As the American government's best insight into the thinking of and orders from Mr. Putin, the source was also key to the C.I.A.'s assessment that he affirmatively favored Donald J. Trump's election and personally ordered the hacking of the Democratic National Committee.

The informant, according to people familiar with the matter, was outside of Mr. Putin's inner circle, but saw him regularly and had access to high-level Kremlin decision-making — easily making the source one of the agency's most valuable assets.

Handling and running a Moscow-based informant is extremely difficult because of Mr. Putin's counterintelligence defenses. The Russians are known to make life miserable for foreign spies, following them constantly and at times roughing them up. Former C.I.A. employees describe the entanglements as "Moscow rules."

The informant's information was so delicate, and the need to protect the source's identity so important, that the C.I.A. director at the time, John O. Brennan, kept information from the operative out of President Barack Obama's daily brief in 2016. Instead, Mr. Brennan sent separate intelligence reports, many based on the source's information, in special sealed envelopes to the Oval Office.

The information itself was so important and potentially contentious in 2016 that top C.I.A. officials ordered a full review of the informant's record, according to people briefed on the matter. Officials reviewed information the source had provided years earlier to ensure that it had proved accurate.

Even though the review passed muster, the source's rejection of the C.I.A.'s initial offer of exfiltration prompted doubts among some counterintelligence officials. They wondered whether the informant had been turned and had become a double agent, secretly betraying his American handlers. That would almost certainly mean that some of the information the informant provided about the Russian interference campaign or Mr. Putin's intentions would have been inaccurate.

Some operatives had other reasons to suspect the source could be a double agent, according to two former officials, but they declined to explain further.

Other current and former officials who acknowledged the doubts said they were put to rest when the source agreed to be extracted after the C.I.A. asked a second time.

Leaving behind one's native country is a weighty decision, said Joseph Augustyn, a former senior C.I.A. officer who once ran the agency's defector resettlement center. Often, informants have kept their spy work secret from their families.

"It's a very difficult decision to make, but it is their decision to make," Mr. Augustyn said. "There have been times when people have not come out when we strongly suggested that they should."

The decision to extract the informant was driven "in part" because of concerns that Mr. Trump and his administration had mishandled delicate intelligence, CNN reported. But former intelligence officials said there was no public evidence that Mr. Trump directly endangered the source, and other current American officials insisted that media scrutiny of the agency's sources alone was the impetus for the extraction.

Mr. Trump was first briefed on the intelligence about Russian interference, including material from the prized informant, two weeks before his inauguration. A C.I.A. spokeswoman responding to the CNN report called the assertion that Mr. Trump's handling of intelligence drove the reported extraction "misguided speculation."

Some former intelligence officials said the president's closed-door meetings with Mr. Putin and other Russian officials, along with Twitter posts about delicate intelligence matters, have sown concern among overseas sources.

"We have a president who, unlike any other president in modern history, is willing to use sensitive, classified intelligence however he sees fit," said Steven L. Hall, a former C.I.A. official who led the agency's Russia operations. "He does it in front of our adversaries. He does it by tweet. We are in uncharted waters."

But the government had indicated that the source existed long before Mr. Trump took office, first in formally accusing Russia of interference in October 2016 and then when intelligence officials declassified parts of their assessment about the interference campaign for public release in January 2017. News agencies, including NBC, began reporting around that time about Mr. Putin's involvement in the election sabotage and on the C.I.A.'s possible sources for the assessment.

The following month, The Washington Post reported that the C.I.A.'s conclusions relied on "sourcing deep inside the Russian government." And The New York Times later published articles disclosing details about the source.

The news reporting in the spring and summer of 2017 convinced United States government officials that they had to update and revive their extraction plan, according to people familiar the matter.

The extraction ensured the informant was in a safer position and rewarded for a long career in service to the United States. But it came at a great cost: It left the C.I.A. struggling to understand what was going on inside the highest ranks of the Kremlin.

The agency has long struggled to recruit sources close to Mr. Putin, a former intelligence officer himself wary of C.I.A. operations. He confides in only a small group of people and has rigorous operational security, eschewing electronic communications.

James R. Clapper Jr., the former director of national intelligence who left office at the end of the Obama administration, said he had no knowledge of the decision to conduct an extraction. But, he said, there was little doubt that revelations about the extraction were "going to make recruiting assets in Russia even more difficult than it already is."

Top Secret Russian Unit Seeks to Destabilize Europe, Security Officials Say

BY MICHAEL SCHWIRTZ | OCT. 8, 2019

FIRST CAME A destabilization campaign in Moldova, followed by the poisoning of an arms dealer in Bulgaria and then a thwarted coup in Montenegro. Last year, there was an attempt to assassinate a former Russian spy in Britain using a nerve agent. Though the operations bore the fingerprints of Russia's intelligence services, the authorities initially saw them as isolated, unconnected attacks.

Western security officials have now concluded that these operations, and potentially many others, are part of a coordinated and ongoing campaign to destabilize Europe, executed by an elite unit inside the Russian intelligence system skilled in subversion, sabotage and assassination.

The group, known as Unit 29155, has operated for at least a decade, yet Western officials only recently discovered it. Intelligence officials in four Western countries say it is unclear how often the unit is mobilized and warn that it is impossible to know when and where its operatives will strike.

The purpose of Unit 29155, which has not been previously reported, underscores the degree to which the Russian president, Vladimir V. Putin, is actively fighting the West with his brand of so-called hybrid warfare — a blend of propaganda, hacking attacks and disinformation — as well as open military confrontation.

"I think we had forgotten how organically ruthless the Russians could be," said Peter Zwack, a retired military intelligence officer and former defense attaché at the United States Embassy in Moscow, who said he was not aware of the unit's existence.

In a text message, Dmitri S. Peskov, Mr. Putin's spokesman,

directed questions about the unit to the Russian Defense Ministry. The ministry did not respond to requests for comment.

Hidden behind concrete walls at the headquarters of the 161st Special Purpose Specialist Training Center in eastern Moscow, the unit sits within the command hierarchy of the Russian military intelligence agency, widely known as the G.R.U.

Though much about G.R.U. operations remains a mystery, Western intelligence agencies have begun to get a clearer picture of its underlying architecture. In the months before the 2016 presidential election, American officials say two G.R.U. cyber units, known as 26165 and 74455, hacked into the servers of the Democratic National Committee and the Clinton campaign, and then published embarrassing internal communications.

Last year, Robert S. Mueller III, the special counsel overseeing the inquiry into Russian interference in the 2016 elections, indicted more than a dozen officers from those units, though all still remain at large. The hacking teams mostly operate from Moscow, thousands of miles from their targets.

By contrast, officers from Unit 29155 travel to and from European countries. Some are decorated veterans of Russia's bloodiest wars, including in Afghanistan, Chechnya and Ukraine. Its operations are so secret, according to assessments by Western intelligence services, that the unit's existence is most likely unknown even to other G.R.U. operatives.

The unit appears to be a tight-knit community. A photograph taken in 2017 shows the unit's commander, Maj. Gen. Andrei V. Averyanov, at his daughter's wedding in a gray suit and bow tie. He is posing with Col. Anatoly V. Chepiga, one of two officers indicted in Britain over the poisoning of a former spy, Sergei V. Skripal.

"This is a unit of the G.R.U. that has been active over the years across Europe," said one European security official, who spoke on condition of anonymity to describe classified intelligence matters. "It's been a surprise that the Russians, the G.R.U., this unit, have felt free to go ahead and carry out this extreme malign activity in friendly countries. That's been a shock."

To varying degrees, each of the four operations linked to the unit attracted public attention, even as it took time for the authorities to confirm that they were connected. Western intelligence agencies first identified the unit after the failed 2016 coup in Montenegro, which involved a plot by two unit officers to kill the country's prime minister and seize the Parliament building.

But officials began to grasp the unit's specific agenda of disruption only after the March 2018 poisoning of Mr. Skripal, a former G.R.U. officer who had betrayed Russia by spying for the British. Mr. Skripal and his daughter, Yulia, fell grievously ill after exposure to a highly toxic nerve agent, but survived.

(Three other people were sickened, including a police officer and a man who found a small bottle that British officials believe was used to carry the nerve agent and gave it to his girlfriend. The girlfriend, Dawn Sturgess, died after spraying the nerve agent on her skin, mistaking the bottle for perfume.)

The poisoning led to a geopolitical standoff, with more than 20 nations, including the United States, expelling 150 Russian diplomats in a show of solidarity with Britain.

Ultimately, the British authorities exposed two suspects, who had traveled under aliases but were later identified by the investigative site Bellingcat as Colonel Chepiga and Alexander Mishkin. Six months after the poisoning, British prosecutors charged both men with transporting the nerve agent to Mr. Skripal's home in Salisbury, England, and smearing it on his front door.

But the operation was more complex than officials revealed at the time.

Exactly a year before the poisoning, three Unit 29155 operatives traveled to Britain, possibly for a practice run, two European officials said. One was Mr. Mishkin. A second man used the alias Sergei Pavlov. Intelligence officials believe the third operative, who used the alias Sergei Fedotov, oversaw the mission.

Soon, officials established that two of these officers — the men using the names Fedotov and Pavlov — had been part of a team that attempted to poison the Bulgarian arms dealer Emilian Gebrev in 2015. (The other operatives, also known only by their aliases, according to European intelligence officials, were Ivan Lebedev, Nikolai Kononikhin, Alexey Nikitin and Danil Stepanov.)

The team would twice try to kill Mr. Gebrev, once in Sofia, the capital, and again a month later at his home on the Black Sea.

Speaking to reporters in February at the Munich Security Conference, Alex Younger, the chief of MI6, Britain's foreign intelligence service, spoke out against the growing Russian threat and hinted at coordination, without mentioning a specific unit.

"You can see there is a concerted program of activity — and, yes, it does often involve the same people," Mr. Younger said, pointing specifically to the Skripal poisoning and the Montenegro coup attempt. He added: "We assess there is a standing threat from the G.R.U. and the other Russian intelligence services and that very little is off limits."

The Kremlin sees Russia as being at war with a Western liberal order that it views as an existential threat.

At a ceremony in November for the G.R.U.'s centenary, Mr. Putin stood beneath a glowing backdrop of the agency's logo — a red carnation and an exploding grenade — and described it as "legendary." A former intelligence officer himself, Mr. Putin drew a direct line between the Red Army spies who helped defeat the Nazis in World War II and officers of the G.R.U., whose "unique capabilities" are now deployed against a different kind of enemy.

"Unfortunately, the potential for conflict is on the rise in the world," Mr. Putin said during the ceremony. "Provocations and outright lies are being used and attempts are being made to disrupt strategic parity."

In 2006, Mr. Putin signed a law legalizing targeted killings abroad, the same year a team of Russian assassins used a radioactive isotope to murder Aleksander V. Litvinenko, another former Russian spy, in London.

Unit 29155 is not the only group authorized to carry out such operations, officials said. The British authorities have attributed Mr. Litvinenko's killing to the Federal Security Service, the intelligence agency once headed by Mr. Putin that often competes with the G.R.U.

Although little is known about Unit 29155 itself, there are clues in public Russian records that suggest links to the Kremlin's broader hybrid strategy.

A 2012 directive from the Russian Defense Ministry assigned bonuses to three units for "special achievements in military service." One was Unit 29155. Another was Unit 74455, which was involved in the 2016 election interference. The third was Unit 99450, whose officers are believed to have been involved in the annexation of the Crimean Peninsula in 2014.

A retired G.R.U. officer with knowledge of Unit 29155 said that it specialized in preparing for "diversionary" missions, "in groups or individually — bombings, murders, anything."

"They were serious guys who served there," the retired officer said. "They were officers who worked undercover and as international agents."

Photographs of the unit's dilapidated former headquarters, which has since been abandoned, show myriad gun racks with labels for an assortment of weapons, including Belgian FN-30 sniper rifles, German G3A3s, Austrian Steyr AUGs and American M16s. There was also a form outlining a training regimen, including exercises for hand-to-hand combat. The retired G.R.U. officer confirmed the authenticity of the photographs, which were published by a Russian blogger.

The current commander, General Averyanov, graduated in 1988 from the Tashkent Military Academy in what was then the Soviet Republic of Uzbekistan. It is likely that he would have fought in both the first and second Chechen wars, and he was awarded a Hero of Russia medal, the country's highest honor, in January 2015. The two officers charged with the Skripal poisoning also received the same award.

Though an elite force, the unit appears to operate on a shoestring budget. According to Russian records, General Averyanov lives in a run-down Soviet-era building a few blocks from the unit's headquarters and drives a 1996 VAZ 21053, a rattletrap Russia-made sedan. Operatives often share cheap accommodation to economize while on the road. British investigators say the suspects in the Skripal poisoning stayed in a low-cost hotel in Bow, a downtrodden neighborhood in East London.

But European security officials are also perplexed by the apparent sloppiness in the unit's operations. Mr. Skripal survived the assassination attempt, as did Mr. Gebrev, the Bulgarian arms dealer. The attempted coup in Montenegro drew an enormous amount of attention, but ultimately failed. A year later, Montenegro joined NATO. It is possible, security officials say, that they have yet to discover other, more successful operations.

It is difficult to know if the messiness has bothered the Kremlin. Perhaps, intelligence experts say, it is part of the point.

"That kind of intelligence operation has become part of the psychological warfare," said Eerik-Niiles Kross, a former intelligence chief in Estonia. "It's not that they have become that much more aggressive. They want to be felt. It's part of the game."

Vast Dragnet Targets Theft of Biomedical Secrets for China

BY GINA KOLATA | NOV. 4, 2019

Nearly 200 investigations are underway at major academic centers. Critics fear that researchers of Chinese descent are being unfairly targeted.

THE SCIENTIST AT M.D. Anderson Cancer Center in Houston was hardly discreet. "Here is the bones and meet of what you want," he wrote in a misspelled email to researchers in China.

Attached was a confidential research proposal, according to administrators at the center. The scientist had access to the document only because he had been asked to review it for the National Institutes of Health — and the center had examined his email because federal officials had asked them to investigate him.

The N.I.H. and the F.B.I. have begun a vast effort to root out scientists who they say are stealing biomedical research for other countries from institutions across the United States. Almost all of the incidents they uncovered and that are under investigation involve scientists of Chinese descent, including naturalized American citizens, allegedly stealing for China.

Seventy-one institutions, including many of the most prestigious medical schools in the United States, are now investigating 180 individual cases involving potential theft of intellectual property. The cases began after the N.I.H., prompted by information provided by the F.B.I., sent 18,000 letters last year urging administrators who oversee government grants to be vigilant.

So far, the N.I.H. has referred 24 cases in which there may be evidence of criminal activity to the inspector general's office of the Department of Health and Human Services, which may turn over the cases for criminal prosecution. "It seems to be hitting every discipline in biomedical research," said Dr. Michael Lauer, deputy director for extramural research at the N.I.H.

The investigations have fanned fears that China is exploiting the relative openness of the American scientific system to engage in whole-sale economic espionage. At the same time, the scale of the dragnet has sent a tremor through the ranks of biomedical researchers, some of whom say ethnic Chinese scientists are being unfairly targeted for scrutiny as Washington's geopolitical competition with Beijing intensifies.

"You could take a dart board with medical colleges with significant research programs and, as far as I can tell, you'd have a 50-50 chance of hitting a school with an active case," said Dr. Ross McKinney Jr., chief scientific officer of the Association of American Medical Colleges.

The alleged theft involves not military secrets, but scientific ideas, designs, devices, data and methods that may lead to profitable new treatments or diagnostic tools.

Some researchers under investigation have obtained patents in China on work funded by the United States government and owned by American institutions, the N.I.H. said. Others are suspected of setting up labs in China that secretly duplicated American research, according to government officials and university administrators.

The N.I.H. has not named most of the scientists under investigation, citing due process, and neither have most of the institutions involved. "As with any personnel matter, we typically do not share names or details of affected individuals," said Brette Peyton, a spokeswoman at M.D. Anderson.

But roughly a dozen scientists are known to have resigned or been fired from universities and research centers across the United States so far. Some have declined to discuss the allegations against them; others have denied any wrongdoing.

In several cases, scientists supported by the N.I.H. or other federal agencies are accused of accepting funding from the Chinese government in violation of N.I.H. rules. Some have said that they did not know the arrangements had to be disclosed or were forbidden.

In August, Feng Tao, 48, a chemist at the University of Kansas known as Franklin, was indicted on four counts of fraud for allegedly failing to disclose a full-time appointment at a Chinese university while receiving federal funds.

His lawyer, Peter R. Zeidenberg, declined to comment on Dr. Tao's case but suggested that prosecutors were targeting academics nationwide who had made simple mistakes.

"Professors, they get their summers off," he said in an interview. "Oftentimes they will take appointments in China for the summer. They don't believe they have to report that."

"They next thing you know, they are being charged with wire fraud with 20-year penalties," he added. "It's like, are you kidding me?"

The investigations have left Chinese and Chinese-American academics feeling "that they will be targeted and that they are at risk," said Frank Wu, a law professor at the University of California Hastings School of the Law and former president of the Committee of 100, an organization of prominent Chinese-Americans.

Dr. Wu and other critics said the cases recalled the government's five-year investigation of Wen Ho Lee, a scientist at the Los Alamos National Laboratory who was accused in 1999 of stealing nuclear warhead plans for China and incarcerated for months, only to be freed after the government's case essentially collapsed. He pleaded guilty to a single felony count of mishandling secrets.

More recently, the Justice Department has been forced to drop theft charges against at least four Chinese-American scientists since 2014: two former Eli Lilly scientists in Indiana, a National Weather Service hydrologist in Ohio and a professor at Temple University in Philadelphia. The Justice Department changed its rules in 2016, giving greater oversight over these national security cases to prosecutors in Washington.

But Dr. Lauer and other officials said the investigations into biomedical research have uncovered clear evidence of wrongdoing. In one case at M.D. Anderson, a scientist who had packed a suitcase with computer hard drives containing research data was stopped at the airport on the way to China, Dr. Lauer and officials at the center said.

ERIN SCHAFF/THE NEW YORK TIMES

The F.B.I. director Christopher Wray appearing before the Senate Judiciary Committee on July 23.

Overall, they argued, the cases paint a disturbing picture of economic espionage in which the Chinese government has been taking advantage of a biomedical research system in the United States built on trust and the free exchange of ideas.

"How would you feel if you were a U.S. scientist sending your best idea to the government in a grant application, and someone ended up doing your project in China?" Dr. McKinney asked.

'THIS WAS SOMETHING WE HAD NEVER SEEN.'

Concern at the N.I.H. about the theft of biomedical research stretches back at least to June 2016, when the F.B.I. contacted N.I.H. officials with unusual questions about the American scientific research system.

How did peer review happen? What sort of controls were in place? "They needed to know how our system worked as compared to, say, national defense," Dr. Lauer said.

The F.B.I. declined to discuss ongoing investigations, including why it initiated so many and how targets were selected. But Christopher Wray, director of the F.B.I., told the Senate Judiciary Committee in July that China is using "nontraditional collectors" of intelligence, and is attempting to "steal their way up the economic ladder at our expense."

The F.B.I.'s field office for commercial counterespionage, in Houston, asked administrators from Texas academic and medical centers to attend classified meetings in the summer of 2018 to discuss evidence of intellectual property theft. The administrators were given emergency security clearances and told to sign nondisclosure agreements.

Then, acting on information from the F.B.I. and other sources, the N.I.H. in late August 2018 began sending letters to medical centers nationwide asking administrators to investigate individual scientists.

"This was something we had never seen," Dr. Lauer said. "It took us a while to grasp the seriousness of the problem."

Some of the first inklings of trouble were discovered by administrators at M.D. Anderson, a prominent cancer research and treatment center. Between August 2018 and January 2019, five letters arrived at the center from the N.I.H. asking administrators to investigate the activities of five faculty members.

Dr. Peter Pisters, president of the cancer center, said he and his colleagues reviewed faculty emails, and they turned up disturbing evidence.

Among the redacted emails provided to The New York Times was one by a scientist planning to whisk proprietary test materials to colleagues in China. "I should be able to bring the whole sets of primers to you (if I can figure out how to get a dozen tubes of frozen DNA onto an airplane)," he wrote.

The redacted M.D. Anderson emails also suggest that a scientist at the medical center sent data and research to the Chinese government in exchange for a $75,000 one-year "appointment" under the Thousand Talents Program, which Beijing established a decade ago to recruit scientists to Chinese universities.

Researchers are legally obligated to disclose such payments to the N.I.H. and to their academic institutions, and the scientist had not done so, according to an internal report on the investigation.

Still another scientist at M.D. Anderson had forwarded a confidential research proposal to a contact in China, writing, "Attached please find an application about mitochondrial DNA mutation in tumor development. Please keep it to yourself."

Administrators at M.D. Anderson said three of the scientists had resigned and one had retired. The fifth case involved a scientist whose transgressions may not be serious enough to be fired.

Dr. Xifeng Wu, who left M.D. Anderson and is now dean of the School of Public Health at Zhejiang University in China, declined to comment on the circumstances of her resignation. "I would like to focus on my research," she said.

M.D. Anderson is not the only institution wrestling with possible scientific misconduct.

Last month, two married scientists, Yu Zhou, 49, and Li Chen, 46, who had worked at Nationwide Children's Hospital in Columbus, Ohio, for a decade, were indicted on charges that they stole technology developed at the hospital and used it to apply for Chinese patents and set up biotech companies in China and the United States.

Dr. Zhou's lawyer, Glenn Seiden, said in an email that the couple did not commit any crimes, and that Dr. Zhou is a "trailblazer" in scientific research.

In May, two scientists at Emory University in Atlanta, Dr. Li Xiao-Jiang and Dr. Li Shihua, were fired after administrators discovered that Dr. Li Xiao-Jiang had received funding from China's Thousand Talents Program.

The couple had worked there for more than two decades, researching Huntington's disease. University administrators declined to provide further information.

"They treated us like criminals," Dr. Li Xiao-Jiang said in an interview near Jinan University in southern China, where he and his wife now work. He disputed the suggestion that they had failed to report ties to China.

"Our work is for humanity," Dr. Li Shihua added. "You can't say if I worked in China, I'm not loyal to the U.S."

In July, Dr. Kang Zhang, the former chief of eye genetics at the University of California, San Diego, resigned after local journalists disclosed his involvement with a biotech firm in China that seemed to rely on research he had performed at the university.

Dr. Zhang, also a member of the Thousand Talents Program, did not tell the university about his role. His lawyer, Leo Cunningham, said that Dr. Zhang's suspension was not related to his involvement with the Chinese biotech firm or the program, but instead to his conduct as an investigator in a clinical trial two years earlier.

What is coming to light, Dr. Lauer said, is "a tapestry of incidents."

Start-up companies in China, federal officials say, were founded on scientific and medical technology that the N.I.H. developed with taxpayer money. "We know there are companies formed in China for which we funded the research," Dr. Lauer said.

Some scientists of Chinese descent also secretly received patents in China for research conducted in the United States, according to Dr. Lauer, and some researchers in the Thousand Talents Program signed contracts that require them to provide the Chinese government with confidential results obtained in the United States or other lab discoveries.

"If the N.I.H. funded it, it should be available to U.S. taxpayers," said Dr. McKinney, of the Association of American Medical Colleges. "But if a project is also funded in China, it is moving intellectual property to China."

ESPIONAGE OR RACISM?

Federal and academic officials stress that they are not targeting Chinese researchers on the basis of their ethnicity. But the F.B.I.'s silence regarding how so many investigations began has exacerbated concern that the government's efforts to uncover economic espionage may tar all Chinese and Chinese-American scientists — and make it more difficult to recruit Chinese students and scholars.

"We can't tell who is guilty or innocent, but look at the actual effect on people of Chinese descent," said Mr. Wu, the law professor. "People are living in fear. It is a question of impact rather than intent."

With the Trump administration taking a harder line against China, including imposing tariffs intended to punish violations of intellectual property rights, Mr. Wu sees a sharp reversal in attitudes about China and the Chinese.

"I am getting calls and emails constantly now from ethnic Chinese — even those who are U.S. citizens — who feel threatened," he said. But few are willing to step forward with allegations of discrimination, he added.

To Dr. Lauer, the charges of racism are unfounded. "Not all the foreign influence cases involve China," he said. "But the vast majority do."

The real question, he added, is how to preserve the open exchange of scientific ideas in the face of growing security concerns. At M.D. Anderson, administrators are tightening controls to make data less freely available.

People can no longer use personal laptops on the wireless network. The center has barred the use of flash drives and disabled USB ports. And all of its employees' computers can now be monitored remotely.

The N.I.H. is clamping down, too. It recommends that reviewers of grant applications have limited ability to download or print them. Those traveling to certain regions should use loaner computers, it says, and academic institutions should be alert to frequent foreign travel by scientists, or frequent publishing with colleagues outside the United States.

The National Science Foundation has commissioned an independent scientific advisory group to recommend ways of balancing openness and security, and warned employees that they are prohibited from participating in programs like China's Thousand Talents Program.

The F.B.I. has given research institutions tools to scan emails for keywords in Mandarin that might tip off administrators to breaches, according to Dr. McKinney.

"The effects this will have on long-term, trusting relationships are hard for us to face," he said. "We just are not used to systematic cheating."

JAVIER HERNANDEZ contributed reporting from Beijing.

Former Twitter Employees Charged With Spying for Saudi Arabia

BY KATE CONGER, MIKE ISAAC, KATIE BENNER AND NICOLE PERLROTH

PUBLISHED NOV. 6, 2019 | UPDATED NOV. 8, 2019

The Justice Department's charges raised questions about the security of technology companies.

SAN FRANCISCO — Ali Alzabarah was an engineer who rose through the ranks at Twitter to a job that gave him access to personal information and account data of the social media service's millions of users.

Ahmad Abouammo was a media partnerships manager at the company who could see the email addresses and phone numbers of Twitter accounts.

On Wednesday, the Justice Department accused the two men of using their positions and their access to Twitter's internal systems to aid Saudi Arabia by obtaining information on American citizens and Saudi dissidents who opposed the policies of the kingdom and its leaders.

The two men, Mr. Alzabarah and Mr. Abouammo, were charged with acting as agents of a foreign power inside the United States, in the first complaint of its kind involving Saudis in the country. The case raised questions about the security of American technology companies already under scrutiny for spreading disinformation and influencing public opinion, showing that these firms can be penetrated from the inside as well.

It also underscored the broad effort that Crown Prince Mohammed bin Salman of Saudi Arabia and his close advisers have conducted to silence critics both inside the kingdom and abroad. Jamal Khashoggi, a columnist for The Washington Post who was critical of the way Saudi Arabia is run, was murdered last year by Saudi agents in Istanbul.

Twitter's headquarters in San Francisco. Two former employees were charged Wednesday with exploiting their access to the company's internal systems to help Saudi Arabia.

As part of Saudi Arabia's campaign, its operatives have been active online. Saudi operatives groomed Mr. Alzabarah, and even before the charges were filed on Wednesday, Western intelligence officials had suspected him of spying on user accounts at Twitter to help the Saudi leadership.

Saudi operatives have also used Twitter to harass critics. Twitter has been a popular platform for news in the kingdom since the Arab Spring uprisings began in 2010.

Both Mr. Alzabarah and Mr. Abouammo left Twitter in 2015. On Wednesday, a spokesman for the company said: "We recognize the lengths bad actors will go to try and undermine our service. Our company limits access to sensitive account information to a limited group of trained and vetted employees."

Twitter added that it was committed to protecting those who used the service to talk about freedom and human rights.

The Washington Post earlier reported on the charges.

American companies like Twitter are attractive targets for foreign agents. "The U.S. has such a dominant position in social media and technology that we are a natural target for our enemies and frenemies," said Mark D. Rasch, a former head of the Justice Department's computer crime division. "They will use any means at their disposal to get individuals' data from U.S. companies for their intelligence and, in this case, suppression efforts."

In addition to Mr. Alzabarah and Mr. Abouammo, federal prosecutors charged Ahmed Almutairi, who previously ran a social media marketing company that did work for the Saudi royal family. He and Mr. Alzabarah are Saudi citizens, and Mr. Abouammo is an American, according to the complaint filed by prosecutors.

The communications between the Twitter employees and a Saudi official began in 2014, according to the complaint. Investigators did not contact Twitter until the end of 2015, when they informed executives that the Saudi government was grooming employees to gain information about the company's users.

According to court documents, the Saudi official who developed the Twitter employees was the "secretary general" of a charitable organization owned by a member of Saudi Arabia's royal family. That description pointed to the MiSK Foundation, a technology-focused nonprofit founded by Prince Mohammed.

MiSK is led by Bader Al Asaker, whose title is secretary general. A person familiar with the case said Mr. Al Asaker is the foreign official who reached out to the Twitter employees.

Mr. Alzabarah had joined Twitter in 2013, rising through the engineering division. He had access to users' telephone numbers and internet protocol addresses, which are unique identification numbers for internet-connected devices.

While at Twitter, Mr. Alzabarah had grown increasingly close to Saudi intelligence operatives, Western intelligence officials told company executives. The operatives eventually persuaded him to peer into the accounts of users they sought information on, including dissidents and activists who spoke against the crown, multiple people have told The Times.

Two people familiar with the case said one of the 6,000 Twitter accounts that Mr. Alzabarah had looked at on behalf of Saudi officials in 2015 belonged to Omar Abdulaziz, a prominent Saudi dissident and confidant of Mr. Khashoggi.

Once Twitter was notified of the breach of security, it placed Mr. Alzabarah on administrative leave while it investigated. Though Twitter did not find direct evidence that Mr. Alzabarah had handed data over to the Saudi kingdom, he left the company in December 2015.

Mr. Alzabarah eventually returned to Saudi Arabia, where he joined the MiSK Foundation.

Mr. Almutairi served as an intermediary between Mr. Alzabarah and Saudi officials, according to the complaint. In messages sent to his wife on May 13, 2015, and included in the complaint, Mr. Alzabarah said Mr. Almutairi had asked him to fly to Washington to meet with a director of the private office of a member of the Saudi royal family.

Mr. Alzabarah flew to Washington the next day. While he stayed there for less than 12 hours, he communicated frequently with Mr. Almutairi, the complaint said. Within a week of the meeting, he began gaining access to Twitter user accounts en masse.

Mr. Abouammo, the media partnerships manager at Twitter, also began exploiting his access to user data within a week after meeting with an unnamed Saudi official in London in 2014, according to the complaint. One of the users was a prominent critic of the Saudi royal family and had more than one million followers on Twitter.

Mr. Abouammo looked up the user's email address, according to the complaint. He later got the email addresses and phone numbers of other Saudi critics, the complaint said.

The Saudi government compensated Mr. Abouammo for his work in a series of wire transfers to him and a member of his family, the complaint said. Mr. Abouammo created a limited liability company to receive at least $300,000 from the Saudi government.

Mr. Abouammo quit his job at Twitter in May 2015 but continued to pass on requests to his former colleagues at the behest of the Saudi official, according to the complaint. He moved to Seattle for a marketing job at Amazon but left the company more than a year ago, an Amazon spokesman said. When an F.B.I. agent interviewed him in 2018, he lied to the agent and produced false documents, the complaint said.

Mr. Abouammo was arrested in Seattle on Tuesday, a law enforcement official said.

Saudi Arabia is one of Twitter's five most active markets. In the first six months of 2015, when Mr. Alzabarah is accused of starting to use his access to account information, Twitter received 93 emergency requests for user data from Saudi Arabia, according to a company transparency report.

In Twitter's most recent transparency report, covering the first half of 2019, it did not disclose any information requests from Saudi Arabia.

The Saudi operation to track its critics has only escalated in recent years. In June 2018, Saudi officials hacked into Mr. Abdulaziz's phone using spyware the Saudi government had bought from NSO Group, an Israeli firm, according to researchers at Citizen Lab, a security research lab at the University of Toronto.

Mr. Abdulaziz has sued NSO Group and also sued Twitter two weeks ago, alleging the company failed to inform him that its employee had hacked his account.

"The Saudi regime is trying to silence any voices for freedom or reform," said Alaa Mahajna, a human rights lawyer representing Mr. Abdulaziz in his case against NSO Group.

KATE CONGER, MIKE ISAAC and NICOLE PERLROTH reported from San Francisco, and KATIE BENNER from Washington.

Glossary

agitators People who stir up public feeling on controversial issues.

attaché A person on the staff of an ambassador.

Bolshevist A supporter of the party that seized Russia's government in 1917.

censorship The suppression or redaction of content deemed objectionable or harmful.

centenary The hundredth anniversary of something; a centennial.

cipher A coded message.

classified Secret.

courtesan A sex worker, particularly one who caters to wealthy or high-class clientele.

cryptography Coding and decoding secret messages.

espionage The act of spying.

exfiltration The secret withdrawal of spies or soldiers.

impunity Freedom from harm or punishment.

incendiarism The act of setting a fire intentionally.

intelligence Information of interest to the military or government.

Kremlin The executive branch of Russia's government. It is also the name of the fortified complex in Moscow where the President lives.

Sabbath A day of worship.

saboteurs People who cause damage intentionally.

Media Literacy Terms

"Media literacy" refers to the ability to access, understand, critically assess and create media. The following terms are important components of media literacy, and they will help you critically engage with the articles in this title.

angle The aspect of a news story that a journalist focuses on and develops.

attribution The method by which a source is identified or by which facts and information are assigned to the person who provided them.

balance Principle of journalism that both perspectives of an argument should be presented in a fair way.

bias A disposition of prejudice in favor of a certain idea, person or perspective.

column A type of story that is a regular feature, often on a recurring topic, written by the same journalist, generally known as a columnist.

commentary A type of story that is an expression of opinion on recent events by a journalist generally known as a commentator.

credibility The quality of being trustworthy and believable, said of a journalistic source.

critical review A type of story that describes an event or work of art, such as a theater performance, film, concert, book, restaurant, radio or television program, exhibition or musical piece, and offers critical assessment of its quality and reception.

feature story Article designed to entertain as well as to inform.

human interest story A type of story that focuses on individuals and how events or issues affect their life, generally offering a sense of relatability to the reader.

impartiality Principle of journalism that a story should not reflect a journalist's bias and should contain balance.

intention The motive or reason behind something, such as the publication of a news story.

interview story A type of story in which the facts are gathered primarily by interviewing another person or persons.

motive The reason behind something, such as the publication of a news story or a source's perspective on an issue.

news story An article or style of expository writing that reports news, generally in a straightforward fashion and without editorial comment.

op-ed An opinion piece that reflects a prominent individual's opinion on a topic of interest.

paraphrase The summary of an individual's words, with attribution, rather than a direct quotation of their exact words.

quotation The use of an individual's exact words indicated by the use of quotation marks and proper attribution.

reliability The quality of being dependable and accurate, said of a journalistic source.

rhetorical device Technique in writing intending to persuade the reader or communicate a message from a certain perspective.

source The origin of the information reported in journalism.

style A distinctive use of language in writing or speech; also a news or publishing organization's rules for consistent use of language with regard to spelling, punctuation, typography and capitalization, usually regimented by a house style guide.

tone A manner of expression in writing or speech.

Media Literacy Questions

1. "An Immoral Espionage." (on page 22) and "Custom-House Espionage" (on page 26) are two articles on similar subjects. Do the articles differ in style and tone from one another? Why do you think this is or is not the case?

2. What is the intention of the article "Spies and Their Congeners" (on page 34)? How effectively does it achieve its intended purpose?

3. "Mata Hari, Courtesan and Spy" (on page 46) and "The Women Who Helped America Crack Axis Codes" (on page 174) are critical reviews from different eras. Have journalistic styles changed between both pieces? If they have, why do you think this is?

4. What type of story is "Detectives Begin Cryptography Study" (on page 49)? Can you identify another article in this collection that is the same type of story? What elements helped you come to your conclusion?

5. Analyze the authors' reporting in "Researchers to Permit Pre-publication Review by U.S." (on page 79) and "F.B.I. Said to Have Sent Messages to Spy Suspect" (on page 85). Do you think one journalist is more balanced in their reporting than the other? If so, why do you think so?

6. "E.S. Friedman, 88, Cryptanalyst Who Broke Enemy Codes, Dies" (on page 82) and "Tommy Flowers, 92, Dies; Broke Nazi Codes" (on page 135) are two obituaries on individuals involved with World War

II code breaking. What similarities can you identify between the coverage of both individuals' lives? What are the differences?

7. Does "Biggest Division a Giant Leap in Math" (on page 91) use multiple sources? What are the strengths of using multiple sources in a journalistic piece? What are the weaknesses?

8. Does Janny Scott demonstrate the journalistic principle of impartiality in her article "Alger Hiss, Divisive Icon of the Cold War, Dies at 92" (on page 120)? If so, how did she do so? If not, what could Scott have included to make her article more impartial?

9. Identify the various sources cited in the article "Veiled Messages of Terror May Lurk in Cyberspace" (on page 145). How does Gina Kolata attribute information to each of these sources in her article? How effective are Kolata's attributions in helping the reader identify her sources?

10. The article "What the Country Owes Harriet Tubman" (on page 168) is an example of an op-ed. Identify how Brent Staples's attitude and tone help convey his opinion on the topic.

11. Identify each of the sources in "C.I.A. Informant Extracted From Russia Had Sent Secrets to U.S. for Decades" (on page 187) as a primary source or a secondary source. Evaluate the reliability and credibility of each source. How does your evaluation of each source change your perspective on this article?

12. In "Top Secret Russian Unit Seeks to Destabilize Europe, Security Officials Say" (on page 192), Michael Schwirtz directly quotes Peter Zwack, a retired military intelligence officer and former defense attaché. What are the strengths of the use of a direct quote as opposed to a paraphrase? What are the weaknesses?

Citations

All citations in this list are formatted according to the Modern Language Association's (MLA) style guide.

BOOK CITATION

THE NEW YORK TIMES EDITORIAL STAFF. *Spy Games: Cracking Government Secrets*. New York Times Educational Publishing, 2021.

ONLINE ARTICLE CITATIONS

BARNES, JULIAN E., ET AL. "C.I.A. Informant Extracted From Russia Had Sent Secrets to U.S. for Decades." *The New York Times*, 9 Sept. 2019, https://www.nytimes.com/2019/09/09/us/politics/cia-informant-russia.html.

BUCKLEY, CHRIS, AND EDWARD WONG. "Family of American Imprisoned on Spy Charge in China Appeals for Help." *The New York Times*, 22 Feb. 2019, https://www.nytimes.com/2019/02/22/world/asia/china-american-spying-kai-li.html.

THE CINCINNATI COMMERCIAL. "Execution of Spies at Franklin, Tenn." *The New York Times*, 21 June 1863, https://www.nytimes.com/1863/06/21/archives/execution-of-spies-at-franklin-tenn-interesting-narrative-of-the.html.

CLARK, ALFRED E. "E.S. Friedman, 88, Cryptanalyst Who Broke Enemy Codes, Dies; Broke Bootleggers' Code." *The New York Times*, 3 Nov. 1980, http://timesmachine.nytimes.com/timesmachine/1980/11/03/112167913.html.

THE CLEVELAND LEADER. "Arrest of a Supposed Rebel Spy." *The New York Times*, 19 Feb. 1865, https://www.nytimes.com/1865/02/19/archives/arrest-of-a-supposed-rebel-spy-a-man-in-female-attire.html.

CONGER, KATE, ET AL. "Former Twitter Employees Charged With Spying for Saudi Arabia." *The New York Times*, 6 Nov. 2019, https://www.nytimes.com/2019/11/06/technology/twitter-saudi-arabia-spies.html.

CONKLIN, WILLIAM R. "3 on Trial as Spies Open Defense, Rosenberg Denying All Charges." *The New York Times*, 22 Mar. 1951, https://timesmachine.nytimes.com/timesmachine/1951/03/22/87020212.pdf.

DERI, EMERY. "Spies and Counter-Spies Still Active in Europe." *The New York Times*, 4 Aug. 1929, http://timesmachine.nytimes.com/timesmachine /1929/08/04/91975211.html.

FITZSIMMONS, EMMA G. "Alan Turing, Enigma Code-Breaker and Computer Pioneer, Wins Royal Pardon." *The New York Times*, 24 Dec. 2013, https:// www.nytimes.com/2013/12/24/world/europe/alan-turing-enigma-code -breaker-and-computer-pioneer-wins-royal-pardon.html.

GLANZ, JAMES. "Cryptologists Discover Flaw In E-Mail Security Program." *The New York Times*, 21 Mar. 2001, https://www.nytimes.com/2001/03/21 /us/cryptologists-discover-flaw-in-e-mail-security-program.html.

GOLDSTEIN, RICHARD. "Tommy Flowers, 92, Dies; Broke Nazi Codes." *The New York Times*, 8 Nov. 1998, https://www.nytimes.com/1998/11/08/world /tommy-flowers-92-dies-broke-nazi-codes.html.

GORDON, MERYL. "The Women Who Helped America Crack Axis Codes." *The New York Times*, 6 Nov. 2017, https://www.nytimes.com/2017/11/06 /books/review/liza-mundy-code-girls-world-war-ii.html.

GRIMES, WILLIAM. "Cracking Codes Through the Centuries." *The New York Times*, 3 Feb. 2015, https://www.nytimes.com/2015/02/04/arts/decoding -the-renaissance-at-the-folger-shakespeare.html.

KOLATA, GINA. "The Assault on 114,381,625,757,888,867,669,235,779,976,146,612, 010,218,296,721,242,362,562,561,842,935,706,935,245,733,897,830,597,123,563, 958,705,058,989,075,147,599,290,026,879,543,541." *The New York Times*, 22 Mar. 1994, https://www.nytimes.com/1994/03/22/science/assault.html.

KOLATA, GINA. "Biggest Division a Giant Leap in Math." *The New York Times*, 20 June 1990, https://www.nytimes.com/1990/06/20/us/biggest-division -a-giant-leap-in-math.html.

KOLATA, GINA. "Tied Up in Knots, Cryptographers Test Their Limits." *The New York Times*, 13 Oct. 1991, https://www.nytimes.com/1991/10/13 /weekinreview/ideas-trends-tied-up-in-knots-cryptographers-test-their -limits.html.

KOLATA, GINA. "Vast Dragnet Targets Theft of Biomedical Secrets for China." *The New York Times*, 4 Nov. 2019, https://www.nytimes.com/2019/11/04 /health/china-nih-scientists.html.

KOLATA, GINA. "Veiled Messages of Terror May Lurk in Cyberspace." *The New York Times*, 30 Oct. 2001, https://www.nytimes.com/2001/10/30 /science/veiled-messages-of-terror-may-lurk-in-cyberspace.html.

LEWIS, PETER H. "Attention Shoppers: Internet Is Open." *The New York Times*,

12 Aug. 1994, https://timesmachine.nytimes.com/timesmachine/1994/08/12/934909.html.

LINDSEY, ROBERT. "Californian Is Given 40 Years for Spying." *The New York Times*, 13 Sept. 1977, https://www.nytimes.com/1977/09/13/archives/californian-is-given-40-years-for-spying-sold-the-russians-secrets.html.

MACFARQUHAR, NEIL. "Russia Says He's a Spy. His Lawyer Says He Just Wanted Photos of a Cathedral." *The New York Times*, 22 Jan. 2019, https://www.nytimes.com/2019/01/22/world/europe/russia-paul-whelan.html.

MARKOFF, JOHN. "Code Set Up to Shield Privacy of Cellular Calls Is Breached." *The New York Times*, 20 Mar. 1997, https://www.nytimes.com/1997/03/20/business/code-set-up-to-shield-privacy-of-cellular-calls-is-breached.html.

MARKOFF, JOHN. "Codebook Shows an Encryption Form Dates Back to Telegraphs." *The New York Times*, 25 July 2011, https://www.nytimes.com/2011/07/26/science/26code.html.

MARKOFF, JOHN. "Cryptography Pioneers Win Turing Award." *The New York Times*, 1 Mar. 2016, https://www.nytimes.com/2016/03/02/technology/cryptography-pioneers-to-win-turing-award.html.

MARKOFF, JOHN. "Scientists Expand Scale of Digital Snooping Alert." *The New York Times*, 4 Sept. 2013, https://www.nytimes.com/2013/09/05/technology/researchers-develop-digital-eavesdropping-alarm.html.

MINNIGERODE, FITZHUGH L. "Mata Hari, Courtesan and Spy." *The New York Times*, 11 May 1930, http://timesmachine.nytimes.com/timesmachine/1930/05/11/97799044.html.

THE NEW YORK TIMES. "British Tell How They Learned Nazi Secrets." *The New York Times,* 10 Nov. 1974, http://timesmachine.nytimes.com/timesmachine/1974/11/10/87606757.html.

THE NEW YORK TIMES. "Coding Techniques Are Detailed at Navy Spy Trial." *The New York Times*, 27 Mar. 1986, https://www.nytimes.com/1986/03/27/us/coding-techniques-are-detailed-at-navy-spy-trial.html.

THE NEW YORK TIMES. "Custom-House Espionage." *The New York Times*, 15 July 1881, http://timesmachine.nytimes.com/timesmachine/1881/07/15/98565347.html.

THE NEW YORK TIMES. "A Cryptic Ploy in Cryptography." *The New York Times*, 29 Oct. 1977, https://www.nytimes.com/1977/10/29/archives/a-cryptic-ploy-in-cryptography.html.

THE NEW YORK TIMES. "Danger from Spies and Traitors." *The New York Times*, 2 Mar. 1862, https://www.nytimes.com/1862/03/02/archives/danger-from-spies-and-traitors.html.

THE NEW YORK TIMES. "Detectives Begin Cryptography Study." *The New York Times*, 12 Feb. 1935, http://timesmachine.nytimes.com/timesmachine /1935/02/12/93451454.html.

THE NEW YORK TIMES. "An Immoral Espionage." *The New York Times*, 5 Feb. 1890, http://timesmachine.nytimes.com/timesmachine/1880 /02/05/98884275.html.

THE NEW YORK TIMES. "The Inventor of the Code of Army Signals." *The New York Times*, 14 Feb. 1862, http://timesmachine.nytimes.com/timesmachinc /1862/02/14/78678449.html.

THE NEW YORK TIMES. "Secret Cable Code for World's Police." *The New York Times*, 14 Jan. 1925, http://timesmachine.nytimes.com/timesmachine/1925 /01/14/101632586.html.

THE NEW YORK TIMES. "Spies and Their Congeners." *The New York Times*, 22 Apr. 1922, http://timesmachine.nytimes.com/timesmachine/1918/04 /22/102694493.html.

THE NEW YORK TIMES. "Suffragette Cipher." *The New York Times*, 7 Apr. 1912, http://timesmachine.nytimes.com/timesmachine/1912/04/07/100358951 .html.

THE NEW YORK TIMES. "The Victories of the Spy." *The New York Times*, 3 Nov. 1917, http://timesmachine.nytimes.com/timesmachine /1917/11/03/102374411.html.

PURDUM, TODD S. "Code Talkers' Story Pops Up Everywhere." *The New York Times*, 11 Oct. 1999, https://www.nytimes.com/1999/10/11/us/code-talkers -story-pops-up-everywhere.html.

RASKIN, A. H. "Story of the Rosenbergs: Two Links in Atomic Conspiracy." *The New York Times*, 21 June 1953, http://timesmachine.nytimes.com /timesmachine/1953/06/21/92719704.html.

ROTHSTEIN, EDWARD. "Security Secrets, Dated but Real." *The New York Times*, 1 Aug. 2014, https://www.nytimes.com/2014/08/02/arts/design /national-cryptologic-museum-is-the-nsas-public-face.html.

SCHWIRTZ, MICHAEL. "Top Secret Russian Unit Seeks to Destabilize Europe, Security Officials Say." *The New York Times*, 8 Oct. 2019, https://www .nytimes.com/2019/10/08/world/europe/unit-29155-russia-gru.html.

SCOTT, JANNY. "Alger Hiss, Divisive Icon of the Cold War, Dies at 92." *The New York Times*, 16 Nov. 1996, https://www.nytimes.com/1996/11/16/nyregion /alger-hiss-divisive-icon-of-the-cold-war-dies-at-92.html.

SEVERO, RICHARD. "Researchers to Permit Pre-Publication Review by U.S." *The New York Times*, 1 Nov. 1980, http://timesmachine.nytimes.com /timesmachine/1980/11/01/112163889.html.

SHENON, PHILIP. "F.B.I. Said to Have Sent Messages to Spy Suspect." *The New York Times*, 13 Aug. 1985, https://timesmachine.nytimes.com /timesmachine/1985/08/13/187633.html.

STAPLES, BRENT. "What the Country Owes Harriet Tubman." *The New York Times*, 17 July 2015, https://takingnote.blogs.nytimes.com/2015/07/17 /what-the-country-owes-harriet-tubman/.

WEINER, TIM. "Why I Spied: Aldrich Ames." *The New York Times*, 31 July 1994, https://www.nytimes.com/1994/07/31/magazine/why-i-spied-aldrich -ames.html.

WILFORD, JOHN NOBLE. "Science Agency Blocks Funds to Aid Research on Computer Coding." *The New York Times*, 27 Aug. 1980, http://timesmachine .nytimes.com/timesmachine/1980/08/27/111281840.html.

Index

RSA 129, 99–104

S

Sanger, David E., 187–191

Schneier, Bruce, 132, 134,
144, 147

Schwartz, Daniel, 80

Schwirtz, Michael, 192–197

Scott, Janny, 120–129

Severo, Richard, 79–81

Shamir, Adi, 96–97, 98, 100

Shenon, Philip, 85–87

Sherman, Bill, 164

Shields, Andrew, 154, 155

Sigaba encryption
machine, 163, 164, 166

Simmons, Gus, 92, 93

Snowden, Edward, 153,
158, 159, 172

Sobell, Morton, 50, 51, 56,
63, 64

Society for the Prevention
of Crime, 22–25

Staples, Brent, 168–170

steganography, 145–149,
165

Strassnoff, Ignatius, 44

T

Trump, Donald/Trump
administration, 184, 185,
186, 188, 189–190, 205

Tubman, Harriet, 142,

168–170

Turing, Alan, 156–157, 171

Turing Award, 171–173

Twitter, 9, 190, 207–211

U

Ultra, 66–69

Unit 29155, 192–197

V

Venona project, 151

Volkogonov, Dmitri, 128

Votruba, Miroslav, 143

W

Wagner, David, 131, 132

Walker, John A., Jr., 85, 86,
87, 89, 90

Weiner, Tim, 105–115

Weinstein, Allen, 125,
126–127, 129

Wheeler, Thomas E., 133

Whelan, Paul N., 179–181

Whitney, D. J., 22–25

Whitworth, Jerry A., 85,
88–90

Wilford, John Noble, 75–78

Williams, Lawrence,
execution of, 14–19

Women's Social and Polit-
ical Union, telegraphic
code of, 30–31

Wong, Edward, 182–186

Woolsey, R. James, 105, 107

World War I, 7, 30, 38, 41,
82, 150, 159, 165, 166
post-war espionage,
38–45
spies and traitors in
America, 32–33, 34–35

World War II, 7, 50, 66–69,
73, 82, 135–137, 142,
146–147, 151, 161, 165, 195
American female code
breakers, 174–178
Colossus, 135, 136–137
Enigma machine, 7, 50,
67, 68, 135, 137, 156–157,
158, 159, 162, 163, 164,
166, 176
Lorenz machines, 135,
136, 137
Navajo Code Talkers,
138–141
Ultra, 66–69

Wray, Christopher, 202

Wu, Frank, 200, 205

Y

Yakovlev, Anatoli A., 51,
60–61

Z

Zhang, Kang, 204

Zimmermann, Philip R.,
119

This book is current up until the time of printing. For the most up-to-date reporting, visit www.nytimes.com.